Nostalgic Branding in the Toy Industry

In recent years, there has been a clear tendency to undertake marketing initiatives that appeal to consumers' emotions, experiences, and memories. This book explores the essence of nostalgic branding by presenting the concept of nostalgia, analysing nostalgic attitudes and consumer behaviour, and illustrating how to position nostalgic brands using the toy market as an example.

The book explores the role nostalgia plays in our lives, what types of nostalgic brands we find on the market, how nostalgia influences consumer attitudes and behaviour, and how to position brands using nostalgia. It shows readers how memories influence their behaviour and provides managers with insights on how to successfully manage nostalgic brands, not only in the toy industry. Using their own research results, the authors demonstrate how to use the fundamental emotion known as nostalgia for successful brand positioning.

Nostalgic Branding in the Toy Industry is addressed primarily to scholars and doctoral students conducting research in the area of brand management, marketing, and consumer behaviour.

Kamil Lubiński is an assistant professor at the Institute of Marketing and Sustainable Development, Faculty of Organization and Management at Lodz University of Technology (Poland). He is a graduate of the 'Linguistics for Business' programme at the University of Lodz and the 'Management' programme at IFE, Lodz University of Technology. He has authored scientific publications focusing on nostalgic brand positioning, with a particular interest in this marketing phenomenon within the games and toys market.

Magdalena Grębosz-Krawczyk is a researcher, educator, and marketing specialist. She is the head of the marketing department at Lodz University of Technology (Poland). Her research focuses on brand management, with particular emphasis on creating brand images on social media and nostalgic branding. She has authored over 150 scientific publications. She successfully manages research projects funded by the Polish Ministry of Science and Higher Education, the Polish National Science Center, the Polish National Agency for International Exchange, and the Embassy of the French Republic. Scholarship holder of the Bekker Programme, she has completed several scientific internships and served as a visiting professor at foreign universities in France, Finland, and Slovakia.

Routledge Focus on Business and Management

The fields of business and management have grown exponentially as areas of research and education. This growth presents challenges for readers trying to keep up with the latest important insights. *Routledge Focus on Business and Management* presents small books on big topics and how they intersect with the world of business research.

Individually, each title in the series provides coverage of a key academic topic, whilst collectively, the series forms a comprehensive collection across the business disciplines.

Digital Transformation of Performing Arts
Trends in the Classical Music Industry
Salvino A. Salvaggio

Globalization and Entrepreneurship
Cases from China, Japan and Bangladesh
Mirjana Radović-Marković, Yao Ouyang, and Md. Shajahan Kabir

Comparative Dynamics in the Comics Industry
Contrasting Cultures in France, Belgium and Netherlands
Rudi de Vries

Reimagining Organizational Change
Richard J. Badham and Brenda M. Santiago

Nostalgic Branding in the Toy Industry
Kamil Lubiński and Magdalena Grębosz-Krawczyk

For more information about this series, please visit: www.routledge.com/Routledge-Focus-on-Business-and-Management/book-series/FBM

Nostalgic Branding in the Toy Industry

Kamil Lubiński and Magdalena Grębosz-Krawczyk

Routledge
Taylor & Francis Group
LONDON AND NEW YORK

First published 2025
by Routledge
4 Park Square, Milton Park, Abingdon, Oxon OX14 4RN

and by Routledge
605 Third Avenue, New York, NY 10158

Routledge is an imprint of the Taylor & Francis Group, an informa business

British Library Cataloguing-in-Publication Data
A catalogue record for this book is available from the British Library

ISBN: 978-1-032-99799-5 (hbk)
ISBN: 978-1-032-99800-8 (pbk)
ISBN: 978-1-003-60607-9 (ebk)

DOI: 10.4324/9781003606079

Typeset in Times New Roman
by Apex CoVantage, LLC

Contents

List of figures *vi*
List of tables *vii*

Introduction 1

PART I
The conceptual framework of nostalgia in brand management 3

1 The concept of nostalgia in marketing 5

2 Nostalgic branding 24

3 Consumers' motivations and behaviours in the context of nostalgia-oriented purchase 44

PART II
Nostalgic branding in toy industry – research results 65

4 Perception of nostalgic brands in toy industry – results of a qualitative study 67

5 Nostalgia-oriented purchase – results of the quantitative research 99

Final conclusions 129

Appendix *132*

Figures

4.1 The research procedure 68
4.2 Word cloud reflecting the participant's perception of 'Power Rangers' 76
4.3 Word cloud reflecting the participant's perception of 'Barbie' 79
4.4 Word cloud reflecting the participant's perception of 'LEGO' 83
4.5 Word cloud reflecting the participant's perception of 'Transformers' 86
4.6 Word cloud reflecting the participant's perception of 'Pokémon' 90
4.7 Word cloud reflecting the participant's perception of 'My Little Pony' 93
5.1 The conceptualisation of the positioning of a nostalgic toy brand 117
5.2 Forms of storytelling practices in the toy's life cycle 119
5.3 Application of the strategy of 'backward innovation' in the toy industry 121

Tables

1.1	The most significant definitions of nostalgia in social sciences literature	10
1.2	The most significant categorisations of nostalgia in marketing literature	15
2.1	Examples of previous studies of nostalgia in consumer behaviour	33
2.2	The results of systematic literature review on nostalgia in toy industry	37
4.1	Overview of focus group participants	72
4.2	Focal toy manufacturers chosen for the study based on global revenue in 2021 *based on the data obtained from statista.com*	73
4.3	Profiles of focal toy brands	74
5.1	Operationalisation of nostalgia	100
5.2	Operationalisation of gift-giving	101
5.3	Operationalisation of self-gifts	102
5.4	Operationalisation of brand attitude	103
5.5	Types of motivation	103
5.6	Professional situation of respondents	104
5.7	Having an offspring	104
5.8	Nostalgic attitude of customers by gender	105
5.9	Nostalgic attitude of customers by age groups	106
5.10	Gift-giving behaviour during the purchase of a toy by gender	107
5.11	Gift-giving predisposition by age group during toy purchases	107
5.12	Self-gift predisposition during toy purchases by gender	109
5.13	Self-gift predisposition during toy purchases by age groups	109
5.14	Factors affecting purchase decision by gender	110
5.15	Factors affecting purchase decision according to parental status	111
5.16	Overview of motivations' impact on purchasing toys by gender	113
5.17	Overview of motivations' impact on purchasing toys by age group	114

Introduction

In recent years, there has been a noticeable trend towards marketing initiatives that appeal to consumers' emotions, experiences, and memories. Nostalgia serves as a key foundation for building a strong bond between consumers and brands. This book delves into the essence of nostalgic branding by exploring the concept of nostalgia, analysing nostalgic attitudes and consumer behaviour, and demonstrating how to position nostalgic brands, with the toy market as a case study.

Nostalgia, often referred to as a 'yearning for yesterday', is typically defined as a preference for objects or experiences that were prevalent during one's youth. However, it is a more complex and multifaceted concept, extensively explored by only a limited number of researchers. While commonly regarded as an emotion, nostalgia also encompasses cognitive and motivational dimensions. Scholars have examined it from various perspectives but remain divided on its origins and emotional tone. Some argue that nostalgia is primarily negative, marked by a sense of loss for an irretrievable past, while others emphasise its positive aspects, highlighting the joy and comfort it can bring.

In a rapidly changing market, where the pace of life accelerates and feelings of uncertainty grow, nostalgic brands take on a symbolic role. They offer a connection to the past, often linked with feelings of safety and joy. By leveraging storytelling and emotions, nostalgic brands become symbols of the past, evoking positive memories and rekindling a sense of lost joy. Incorporating nostalgia into brand management allows companies to evoke emotions tied to meaningful experiences and sensations for consumers, frequently referencing an idealised personal or historical past.

Several authors suggest that a nostalgic brand strategy relies on the assumption that nostalgia forms the cornerstone of the strong bond between consumers and the brand. Implementing such a strategy enables the creation of a competitive advantage, not only through functional product or service features but also, and more importantly, through emotional benefits. In this context, a nostalgic brand reflects symbolic benefits, offering added value tied to the symbolism of the past, historical connections with consumers, and associations with the user's past identity and sentimental characteristics. Consumers often gravitate towards products and brands they associate with

DOI: 10.4324/9781003606079-1

fond memories from the past. Consequently, nostalgia is a powerful tool in marketing, utilised by both long-established brands and those successfully relaunched.

This monograph seeks to provide a comprehensive assessment of the impact of nostalgia on brand positioning on the example of the toy industry, with a focus on brand perception and consumer motivations.

The motivation for exploring the impact of nostalgia on brand positioning in the toy industry stems from a significant gap in both theoretical and empirical research. Previous studies have primarily focused on the role of nostalgia in advertising or its use in building a trustworthy brand image with a proven history. While toys are recognised as one of the most nostalgic tangible products regularly purchased, little is known about the factors driving purchase decisions and the motivations behind acquiring nostalgic toys. Addressing this gap is essential for expanding the understanding of nostalgic branding within this context.

The book consists of two parts. The first section of this book delves into the history and concept of nostalgia within the social sciences, its application in marketing and brand management, and its influence on consumer behaviour. This exploration of nostalgia – its types, definitions, and interpretations from both objective and subjective perspectives – serves as a foundation for understanding nostalgic branding. Additionally, it examines the motivations behind consumers' preferences for nostalgic brands, emphasising the critical role of emotional factors in shaping their decision-making processes. The second section of this monograph combines existing research on brand positioning with the authors' findings from qualitative and quantitative studies. This part presents the results of both research phases, demonstrating how nostalgia can be strategically utilised by toy companies to enhance brand perception. The findings offer valuable insights, addressing the need for deeper investigation into the relationship between nostalgic positioning and consumers' emotional reactions to products. Additionally, the authors provide practical recommendations for developing effective brand positioning strategies in the toy industry, grounded in the study's outcomes.

After reading this book, you will gain an understanding of what nostalgia is, the role it plays in our lives, the types of nostalgic brands on the market, how nostalgia impacts consumer attitudes and behaviour, and how to effectively position brands using nostalgia. This book explores how memories shape consumer behaviour and offers valuable insights for managers on managing nostalgic brands successfully, extending beyond the toy industry.

Drawing on their own research, the authors illustrate how the fundamental emotion of nostalgia can be harnessed for effective brand positioning. This book is primarily intended for scientists and doctoral students researching brand management. It also serves as a practical guide for readers and professionals interested in all aspects of nostalgic branding, offering insights into its principles and applications, with a particular focus on the toy industry.

Part I

The conceptual framework of nostalgia in brand management

Introduction to Part I

What is nostalgia, and how can it be understood? How does nostalgia influence modern consumers and, consequently, brand management? There is growing evidence that nostalgia plays a crucial role in people's lives. To date, marketing researchers have focused on studying the antecedents of nostalgia and its consequences in terms of consumer behaviour. Some have highlighted the utility of evoking nostalgia for predicting consumer behaviour. Nostalgic narratives are often perceived as affectively positive, with nostalgic intensity increasing when accompanied by expressions of tenderness and elation. An alternative explanation for the emergence of nostalgia as a dominant societal theme is provided by some authors, who suggest that nostalgia increases as consumers become dissatisfied with contemporary life. Thus, nostalgia can be seen as a coping mechanism in difficult economic times.

Some authors have considered strategies for nostalgic branding to be based on the assumption that nostalgia forms the cornerstone of the strong bond between consumers and brands. Implementing a nostalgic branding strategy enables companies to build a competitive advantage not only through the functional features of products or services but also, more importantly, through emotional benefits. In this context, a nostalgic brand reflects the symbolic benefits it offers.

A nostalgic brand provides added value related to the symbolism of the past, historical connections with consumers, users' past identities, and sentimental personality traits.

This presentation of the phenomenon of nostalgia – its types, definitions, and conceptualisations in both objective and subjective dimensions – aims to serve as an introduction to the topic of nostalgic branding. Therefore, the first part of this book explores the history and concept of nostalgia in the social sciences, its role in marketing and brand management, and its impact on consumer motivations.

In the literature, several attitudinal and behavioural theories and models, such as the Theory of Planned Behaviour (TPB), the Theory of Reasoned

DOI: 10.4324/9781003606079-2

Action (TRA), the Howard Sheth Model (HSM), the Nicosia Model (NM), the Engel-Kollat-Blackwell Model (EKBM), and the Engel-Blackwell-Miniard Model (EBMM), have been extensively used to describe consumers' attitudes and behaviours. One of the key assumptions of TPB, TRA, and HSM is that consumers are rational in their decision-making processes, allowing cognitive approaches to predict behaviour. However, many researchers have criticised these theoretical models for being overly limited in explaining the affective aspects of behaviour. Consequently, the addition of affective variables has been recommended as a valuable extension to these theories. This critique is especially relevant given previous research on nostalgic brands. For this reason, this part also presents consumers' motivations related to their choices of nostalgic brands, highlighting the importance of affective factors in understanding their decision-making processes.

1 The concept of nostalgia in marketing

1.1 Origin and evolution of the concept of nostalgia

The term 'nostalgia', in a form we know from dictionaries, was coined by Hofer in 1688.[1] Given the roots of the Greek words *nostos* and *algos*, nostalgia was meant to describe an innate pain caused by passionate longing for a homeland. However, none of these words conveyed much from its etymological ancestor, apart from emphasising the act of reminiscing a vernacular place. *Nostimon*, as portrayed by Homer, had by no means been associated with sorrow and suffering. It had encapsulated an extraordinary human ability to draw strength and motivation from feelings surrounding the closest ones. Linguistically speaking, it is undeniable that the concept of nostalgia is ambiguous, as it provides incoherent definitions surrounding two opposite feelings. Unfortunately, many researchers do not pay attention to these tiny details, as they usually confuse Hofer's *nostalgos* with Homer's *nostimon*.[2]

Metaphorically speaking, the genesis of nostalgia can be attributed to the biblical account of Adam and Eve. Following their expulsion from paradise, they likely began to look back longingly at what they had lost. Since then, humanity has been plagued by a yearning desire to reclaim a past dear to the heart.[3]

The theme of nostalgia is believed to first appear in Homer's epic 'Odyssey' (c. 800 BC), in which the hero Odysseus cherishes memories of his beloved wife and the city of Ithaca during his ten-year return home from the Trojan War. Although Odysseus often laments that he is far from home, his memories keep his spirits up and spur him on to fight. According to Homer, nostalgia develops a remarkable ability to draw strength and motivation from memories of the past, especially those close to the heart. Nostalgia appeared in the works of many ancient poets, including Euripides, around 400 BC.[4]

In the 17th century, nostalgia was diagnosed by doctors as a medical condition, believing it to be a mental illness with symptoms similar to depression.[5] The theory of nostalgia as a medical condition was developed in Europe. At the time, nostalgia was defined as a physical and emotional upheaval associated with memory functioning and as a 'disorder of the imagination'.[6] One

DOI: 10.4324/9781003606079-3

of the earliest references to nostalgia can be found in the work of a Swiss physician of French origin, Johannes Hofer, who discussed the problem of nostalgia in his doctoral dissertation (dated 1688).[7] Hofer saw nostalgia as a neurological disease originating in the so-called inner brain, where – as it was believed at the time – animal spirits resided. Hofer used the term nostalgia to describe the extreme emotional state experienced by members of the Swiss army who were sent to war far from home. He hypothesised that constantly thinking about the homeland caused the animal spirits in the brain to move. This condition was characterised by feelings of sadness and depression, which, in severe cases, led to suicide attempts. Hofer was considered the first physician to describe nostalgia as a clinical condition.[8] Hofer's key assumption was that the mind can influence the body.[9]

Consequently, from the 17th to 19th centuries, nostalgia was considered an illness, and scholars presented different views on who its victims were and what its symptoms, causes, and treatments were. The association of nostalgia with homesickness has resulted in several groups of theories. In chronological order, these include[10]

- physiological and anatomical theories,
- environmental theories,
- psychological theories,
- theories of instinct,
- combined physiological and psychological theories.

Physiological and anatomical theories addressed the description and interpretation of nostalgia according to Hofer's approach. Representatives of environmental theories tried to explain nostalgia in terms of the environment. In 1731, the German-Swiss physician Scheuchzer stated that nostalgia was the result of a sudden change in climate causing a sharp change in pressure in the human body, which in turn caused blood flow from the heart to the brain, triggering sentimental or nostalgic feelings.[11] Since Swiss soldiers travelled from the mountains to the valleys and back again, this was thought to be the explanation of why this condition only affected members of the Swiss army. Some military doctors believed that the nostalgia was the result of damage to the eardrums and brain caused by the constant ringing of cowbells in the Swiss Alps. However, this theory was disproved when it was discovered that soldiers from other countries, including France and Britain, were also affected by nostalgia.

Guthrie[12] argued that familiar surroundings become part of the personality, and nostalgia arises when an individual is placed in an environment that is foreign to them. Representatives of psychological theories viewed nostalgia as a disturbance of the mind, sometimes resulting in mild or partial insanity. Papillon clearly indicated the symptoms of nostalgia, among which he listed loss of vigour, dementia, anaemia, circulatory disorders, digestive disorders, chills, and fever. Marbe, on the other hand, did not regard nostalgia as an illness but as a mental state characterised by melancholy and even depression.[13] According to Hall's theory, when two conflicting instincts fight for control over an individual, homesickness arises. Hall distinguished between the instinct that predisposed the individual to return home and the instinct that caused the individual to flee.[14]

Summarising psychological theories, Szasz[15] argued that the memory of experiences associated with home could temporarily make an individual unable to function normally away from their homeland. Some authors have proposed a combination of physiological and psychological theories of homesickness. Conklin[16] distinguished between physiological symptoms of nostalgia (e.g., palpitations, high blood pressure, vomiting, diarrhoea, nausea) and psychological symptoms (e.g., tightness in the throat, feelings of loneliness). In contrast, McCann[17] argued that homesickness was physically related to the sympathetic division of the autonomic nervous system, which is activated when an individual has a strong desire to return home that cannot be satisfied. This created a psychological desire that induced feelings of inferiority, fear, and suffering.

In the 19th century, thanks to the intensive development of medicine, concepts began to be precisely defined. The concept of nostalgia became generalised, and the disorder came to the attention of psychiatrists.[18]

Until the mid-20th century, nostalgia was considered a form of melancholy or depression associated with homesickness. However, as the term was 'demilitarised', the meaning of nostalgia changed to a general longing for the past.[19] Nostalgia was no longer just a desire to return home. For people who returned home, they tended to be disappointed, as they did not actually want to return to a place but to a time of their youth. Nevertheless, the occurrence of nostalgia among soldiers in, for example, the United States of America has still been described.[20] In the 20th century, psychologists described nostalgia as an acute longing for a relationship with one's mother, a sad farewell to childhood, a defence against bereavement, or a longing for a past forever lost forever.[21] Nostalgia has been interpreted as an unpleasant state associated with difficulty adjusting or feeling isolated.[22]

Referring to the temporal context, based on literature studies, psychologists Nawas and Platt[23] distinguished nostalgia into past-oriented, present-oriented, and future-oriented.

The first approach, oriented towards the past, is represented by orthodox psychoanalysts who interpret nostalgia as an expression of the desire to return to the source, that is, the state that leads to happiness in the only perfect form we know.[24] A representative of this approach, Martin[25] distinguishes between healthy and pathological nostalgia, noting that true nostalgia, literally and figuratively, requires a healthy surrender of the tendency to return to the past, to our beginnings, to childhood. Past-oriented nostalgia thus involves a desire to return to an earlier period in life.

The second approach to nostalgia is oriented towards the present. Representatives of this approach regard nostalgia primarily as an individual's reaction to an unsuccessful adaptation to the present environment. Rose[26] emphasised the importance of a sense of uncertainty in triggering nostalgia. Lippert,[27] on the other hand, argued that nostalgia results from the discrepancy between the actual and expected images of the environment. Present-tense nostalgia is therefore associated with a reaction resulting from an inability to adapt to the present situation, which involves uncertainty as a trigger for nostalgia.

A future-oriented approach, on the other hand, sees nostalgia as the association of longing with uncertainty of goals and pessimism about future prospects.[28] Future-oriented nostalgia is related to an individual's perception of the future. An individual may be pessimistic (more nostalgic) or optimistic (less nostalgic) about the future.

While researchers in clinical studies of nostalgia focus on the negative symptoms and consequences of nostalgia, psychological studies also point to the benefits of nostalgia. It should be noted at this point that already at the end of the 19th century, the positive aspects of nostalgia were considered by Darwin,[29] and in the 20th century, Werman,[30] Kaplan,[31] and Batcho[32] spoke in a similar vein. Scholars have begun to appreciate and exploit the fact that nostalgia is associated with pleasant memories of the past. Thus, recalling or idealising past experiences can generate positive feelings in the present.[33] Representatives of environmental psychologists[34] confirmed the positive attitude of individuals towards the past expressed in the need to preserve material resources from the past, the appreciation of the past as cultural heritage, the appreciation of one's own past experiences, and a general interest in the past.

In the 1980s, nostalgia became an object of academic interest for researchers working on marketing issues and, in particular, consumer attitudes and behaviour.

1.2 Contemporary concepts of nostalgia

In 1979, Davis, who was the first to describe nostalgia from a sociological point of view, found that many optimistic feelings could be identified in relation to nostalgia. Consequently, nostalgia began to be seen in a more positive light. The results of Davis' survey of university students showed that nostalgia was identified with the words 'warmth', 'good old times', 'childhood', and 'nostalgia', not just 'homesickness'. Thus, nostalgia was reconceptualised and related to any longing for the past. On the basis of empirical findings, Davis defined nostalgia as 'a positively attuned evocation of a relived past', a 'longing for the past', and an 'adoration of the past'.[35] According to the author, nostalgia occurs because people evoke positive memories when experiencing unpleasant moments.

Nostalgia refers to an earlier period in an individual's life and is based on a biased or selective recollection of past experiences. It is interesting to note that the memory of a relived past may not reflect the truth of the events that occurred and may be distorted to form a more positive picture than it actually was.

In addition to defining nostalgia as a longing for the past, Davis[36] distinguished three levels of nostalgia:

- The first level, so-called simple nostalgia, is related to the belief that things were better in the past (i.e., healthier, more beautiful, and more exciting).
- The second level, so-called reflective nostalgia, is related to an evaluation of the past in terms of historical accuracy rather than a sentimental perception of it. Individuals analyse the past but do not glorify it; for example, a person experiencing second-level nostalgia may ask themselves whether everything was as they remember it.
- The third level, so-called interpreted nostalgia, affects the individual who considers the nostalgic experience in terms of the reasons for the nostalgia and its meaning in the context of events in the present, asking themselves why they feel nostalgic.

Contemporary psychologists have confirmed that nostalgia is associated with an increase in positive well-being as a coping mechanism by responding to negative moods with positive memories.[37] The most common feelings associated with nostalgia are joy[38] and sadness.[39] Most research on nostalgia highlights its bipolar, ambivalent nature of nostalgic feelings. Consequently, on the one hand, like other positive emotions, nostalgia can foster social bonds, increase an individual's self-esteem, and thus generate positive mood and well-being. On the other hand, nostalgia can cause sadness, which, according to the authors, is mainly due to the awareness of the impossibility of recalling past events. Nostalgia as an attitude is usually based on reflection and evaluation of the past. It thus contains both a cognitive and an affective component that accompanies reflection and judgement of the past. By their very nature, nostalgic feelings or moods may arise temporarily or be based on a permanent liking for the past.

Many nostalgia researchers emphasise the affective nature of nostalgia and view nostalgia as a temporary but complex emotion.[40]

Consequently, in psychology, nostalgia is often described as an affective-cognitive construct, in which the cognitive component involves remembering, reflecting on, and evaluating things, people, and events from the past, and the affective component describes emotions related to the past.[41]

Although the original concept of nostalgia was related to homesickness, Holbrook and Schindler[42] broadened its meaning by defining nostalgia as a preference (general liking, positive attitude, or positive affect) for objects (people, places, or things) that were more common (popular, fashionable, or used) in earlier years (in early adulthood, adolescence, childhood, and even before the consumer was born). This approach is represented by many researchers and used in marketing. In explaining the concept of nostalgia, both Havlena and Holak[43] and Stern[44] emphasise that nostalgic attitudes can be generated both based on an individual's own past experiences and based on the memories of others from before birth. However, it should be emphasised that nostalgia is not always limited to early adulthood, adolescence, or childhood. Older people may be nostalgic about things and events related to later periods of their lives (e.g., from their children's youth or their grandchildren's childhood).

According to Holbrook and Schindler,[45] nostalgia refers to the experience of objects that have been lost and are no longer available or are difficult to obtain (e.g., the consumer has had to change consumption patterns due to illness, relocation, or natural disaster). However, most authors also relate nostalgia to things known from the past that are available today.

Selected definitions of nostalgia are presented in Table 1.1.

Publications on nostalgia in recent years provide opportunities to make some generalisations about the nature of nostalgic experiences. Nostalgia is most often defined in terms of emotions associated with longing for the past.

If Davis' intention was to provoke the research community to continue what he has started, then he has well succeeded. It is no exaggeration to state that the 1990s have seen a boom in publications covering the issue of nostalgia. Among them, Holbrook and Schindler[46] have viewed nostalgia as 'a preference for objects that were popular when one was younger'. The above definition has confirmed the association between the nostalgic feeling and

Table 1.1 The most significant definitions of nostalgia in social sciences literature

Author(s) and year	*Definition of nostalgia*
Davis (1979)	'A positive evocation of a lived past'.
Belk (1990)	'A wistful mood that may be prompted by an object, a scene, a smell, or a strain of music'.
Holbrook and Schindler (1991)	'A preference toward objects that were common when one was younger'.
Stern (1992)	'An emotional state in which an individual yearns for an idealized or sanitized version of an earlier time period'.
Baker and Kennedy (1994)	'A sentimental bittersweet yearning for an experience, product, or service from the past'.
Sierra and McQuitty (2007)	'An emotion or mood produced by musing about objects, affiliated with a previous time and has the capacity to produce preferences for possessions that generate nostalgic responses'.
Higson (2014)	'A way of relating to a past imagined from the point of view of the present – a response to and re-organization of contemporary experience'.

physical objects of sentimental value. Belk[47] writes that those extraordinary possessions that stir our emotions can create, store, and retrieve a sense of the past that is essential in managing one's identity. In the same vein, Pickering and Keightley[48] have later argued that nostalgia is concerned with the idea of attaining the unattainable, or in other words, to satisfy what has not been ever fulfilled. Tangible preservation of memories connected with a specific episode from one's past, or as Boym[49] has called it, a 'souvenirization of the past', not only delivers a positive perception of the personally experienced past but also compensates for what has been destroyed in the name of deceptive progress. After all, Holak and Havlena[50] conclude that the sentimental feeling does not explain the affection towards those objects, but rather it determines a pattern of preferences for those things that are likely to cast a nostalgic spell. Therefore, nostalgia may be interpreted as a consuming feeling engendered as a response to the fact that time is irreversible.

1.3 Definitions and types of nostalgia in marketing literature

The term nostalgia in a marketing context was defined by Holbrook and Schindler[51] as a preference for items that were more popular during the consumer's youth, adolescence, childhood, or even before birth. In subsequent years, the conceptualisation of nostalgia in marketing was addressed by Havlena and Holak,[52] Stern,[53] Baker and Kennedy,[54] Rousseau and Venter,[55] Goulding,[56] and Pascal et al.[57] An analysis of contemporary definitions of nostalgia used in marketing shows that, despite semantic differences, they generally refer to pleasant feelings or desires associated with objects, persons, or events related to the past.

The most important reasons for the development of nostalgia in marketing include[58]

- a changing demographic structure (an ageing population and consequently an increase in the number of older consumers, more inclined to nostalgia),
- the anxiety and stress of everyday life (a consequence of which is the search for brands that give the feeling of returning to a time when life was simpler and less stressful),
- insecurity caused by political and economic factors (resulting in an intensification of nostalgic attitudes and a return to the brands of the past),
- an increase in the number of brands available on the market (resulting in problems arising in the decision-making process, leading to an easing of decisions by choosing brands that are known and trusted).

Consumer insecurity, linked to the impression of instability and even a feeling of fear and an increase in the level of human sensitivity, can lead to positive consumer attitudes towards brands using nostalgia, retro style, and references to the past. In a postmodern society, the consumer is less and less interested in maximising profit but instead needs a sense of reassurance and trust and wants to enjoy the values offered by brands. The use of nostalgia in marketing helps to create a connection with the past by providing a positive, nostalgic experience.

Key to nostalgia in marketing is the idea of authenticity.[59] Consumers find a sense of authenticity in nostalgic objects and experiences and then use them to construct and validate their own present identity.[60]

According to Belk,[61] it is impossible to understand consumer behaviour without first understanding the meaning consumers attach to specific products and brands. Possessions help the consumer to express and protect his or her present social or ideal self. According to Kleine et al.,[62] consumer goods linked to the past can support the pursuit of independence and uniqueness, as well as the search for belonging and social bonds. The value of a product derives from the importance of the object to the individual.[63] Buyers therefore choose offerings that promise value that is relevant to them, which can be seen not only as the basis for purchasing decisions but also as the outcome of the consumption experience.[64]

Goulding[65] emphasises that strong positive attitudes towards the past can influence attitudes towards certain products and brands with characteristics associated with the past. Although consumers cannot return to the past, they may try to preserve or commemorate the past through nostalgic consumption.[66] Nostalgia can influence buying preferences and behaviour in various ways. On the one hand, consumers may seek products that satisfy their nostalgic needs. In this case, companies that consciously or unconsciously refer to cherished aspects of the past are evaluated by the consumer in terms of their relevance to the current situation. On the other hand, nostalgia can influence the processing of incentives sent by marketers, even if the consumer is not looking for nostalgic products. This means that, in many cases, the consumer encounters products and brands that remind him of the past and thus relate to his nostalgic attitude or activate a momentary feeling of nostalgia, which influences the evaluation of the company's offer. In both cases, nostalgia positively influences the attitude towards the brand.

The use of nostalgia in marketing became common because consumers were dissatisfied with the present or anticipated a bleak future and therefore wanted to return to a more pleasant past. Stern[67] looks for the motivation to purchase products referring to the past in the worship of the old days and admiration for the past. One of the reasons for the occurrence of nostalgia in consumers is also the strong need to confirm the authenticity of products. On the other hand, according to Belk,[68] if the consumer's needs are linked to the past, it becomes the starting point for marketing activities.

Concomitantly, another concept of nostalgia to have made its appearance on the consumer behaviour agenda is authenticity. Some authors understand it as a burning desire for immediate satisfaction. Emmons[69] has defined it as a 'personal striving'. It is because people actively strive to find meaning in their inauthentic lives. Similarly, Beverland and Farrelly[70] have emphasised the loss of fundamental values in the realms of the postmodern world to be the case why consumers so desperately seek authenticity. As has already been discussed, nostalgia is at the nucleus of the concept of inevitable loss. In addition, Belk et al.[71] have acknowledged the phenomenon of 'the fire of desire' as being stimulated by the fear of unfulfillment. Therefore, in longing for what is now regarded to be gone, a subject is longing for what is unattainable. In order to qualify itself as an item of exceptional value, the object must transform its original value into something that makes it even more desirable in the eyes of an individual. Modernity, however, has changed the meaning of the concept of loss for the sake of compensation. Every desire might be replaced by the other one, thereby sustaining within a perpetual cycle of modern consumerism.[72] It could be the reason why Higson[73] writes that modern nostalgia is evident in the sphere of hobbyist activities and collecting. Belk[74] had suggested that such physical (hereby meaning 'authentic') objects connected to the past provide an elusive sense of security, one that makes an individual believe he is by no means abandoned in this world.

Perhaps the most prominent distinction of nostalgia is the one made by Davis between personal and communal nostalgia. The former is associated with a view whereby since people have the ability to reminisce about past events, then it must be a personally remembered past. Those are all the indirect references that make one's memories authentic.[75] Furthermore, there is a strong emotional bond between a personal stance towards this particular past experience and an object owned in the past. As people are getting older, they have a tendency to walk down memory lanes and dive into the times of sweet and innocent youth. Communal nostalgia, on the contrary, occurs on the social level as the consequence of constant changes during the history of a nation.[76] Not only is it a form of collective experience, but it also can be shared among the group members. Kao[77] remarks that although personal nostalgia seems to be a more retrospective and individually based experience, communal nostalgia serves as a tribal totem gathering individuals of the same generation. Along the same lines, Boym[78] has identified reflective and restorative nostalgia. Reflective nostalgia is about a state where a subject longs to return to the past, yet he is aware that he may not stay there due to the irreversibility of time. Furthermore, a person realises that such reflection relies on his own memories. The latter emphasises the glorification of 'a golden age', a time that used to be, and strives to experience it the way it was – to relive those special moments. Capturing the spirit of Davis' work, restorative nostalgia, commonly referred to as 'bad nostalgia', deflates the ability of rational thinking, thereby making it difficult for a person to spot a difference between the illusory projection and the actual reality.

Stern[79] has identified a division between historical and personal nostalgia. The first one is an exaggerated accentuation of the past époque that is so alluring to go there, yet it is unobtainable due to the irreversibility of time. A note of caution is due here since historical nostalgia presents the past time before a person was born. In that case, the main objective is to make consumers believe that a brand is given some unnatural abilities to materialise the objects from the past. Besides, the possession of such goods increases an individual's position within the social hierarchy, as it says much about one's taste for valuable objects. On the contrary, personal nostalgia is precisely what has conceptually remained from 'homesickness' – a 17th-century connotation of a mental disease that had long surrounded the notion of nostalgia. Today, it is way more concerned with the quest for a lost childhood. The view has recently been supported by Kessous and Roux,[80] who have drawn a distinction between long-standing and first-time nostalgia. They are consistent with Stern's writings and, therefore, need no further explanation. No matter whether or not it is the original Stern's or the refreshed Kessous and Roux's re-conceptualisation, both are being used by marketing practitioners. In addition, Grębosz-Krawczyk and Siuda[81] have identified generational and transgenerational nostalgia.

A more complex distinction such as that by Baker and Kennedy[82] has identified three types of nostalgia: real, simulated, and collective. The first captures the spirit of Davis' words on the individualised character of nostalgic reminiscing, namely that the object of wistfulness must be based upon personally experienced past. In other words, this is when an inducement brings about concrete memories associated with the latter, like, for example, an old song being broadcast on the radio. According to Alba and Hutchinson,[83] real nostalgia is pragmatic-based, since to develop a nostalgic reaction, a previous experience that had occurred somewhere in the past is needed. Simulated nostalgia, albeit it does seem like a new concept, in fact, is an updated version of Stern's historical nostalgia. Following Boym's concept,[84] simulated nostalgia, similar to her restorative nostalgia, revolves around the theme of pursuing history. However, though restorative nostalgia does not consider itself to be nostalgic, simulated nostalgia, on the other hand, is.[85] People go to great lengths to recreate the times when they did not live yet wish they could,[86] and it is well noted in marketing research (e.g., Havlena and Holak). Finally, collective nostalgia, just as the Davis' communal one,[87] is concerned with sentimental feelings towards creations of the time, which are movies, songs, and symbols that had been once popular when people were younger and have prevailed to become a celebratory object of a cult. Research suggests some implications regarding the type of products to which preference has been generated by a particular generation. Regardless, Baker and Kennedy[88] advise not to limit collective nostalgia exclusively to generations, as a nation, seen as members of a larger community, might as well qualify.

Higson[89] concludes that not until nostalgia sheds its perception of a singular phenomenon, the concept may not be understood well enough. Routledge,[90] in this regard, claims that it was only in the span of the recent ten to 20 years

Table 1.2 The most significant categorisations of nostalgia in marketing literature

Author(s) and year	*Proposed types of nostalgia*
Davis (1979)	Personal and communal nostalgia
Stern (1992)	Historical and personal nostalgia
Baker and Kennedy (n.d.)	Real, simulated, and collective nostalgia
Boym (2001)	Reflective and restorative nostalgia
Kessous and Roux (2008)	Long-standing and first-time nostalgia
Grębosz-Krawczyk and Siuda (2017)	Generational and transgenerational nostalgia

that nostalgia has come back to the research agenda. Back to Naughton and Vlasic, they have added that later reinterpretations among the next generations have been causing nostalgia to evolve by means of perpetual change within the sphere of its semantic meaning. Therefore, it might be suggested that Davis' view on the 'slow yet steady semantic drift'[91] from medical phenomenon to consumer behaviour does still take place. Wilson[92] writes that despite being a fascinating topic in the research, nostalgia is not an easy concept, for it has been used to describe various things at different times. As a result, some authors in the field (e.g., Pickering and Keightley)[93] have repeatedly complained that Davis' work neatly touched on the phenomenon of nostalgia, thereby overgeneralising the specific ways in which this operates. In fact, he had assumed the role of the psychological mechanisms in determining an individual's proneness towards nostalgic cues, though he had failed to demonstrate whether or not it was the case.[94] Nevertheless, a consensus has been reached that it was a necessary step forward that allowed for such wide reconceptualisation as demonstrated hereinabove.

1.4 Chapter summary

On the basis of the linguistic-functional analysis of the literature, 'nostalgia' carries more significance in its meaning than previously thought in the times of Weltschmerz – unjustly associating it with a psychopathological disorder. In its original sense, *nostos*, the antecedent of today's nostalgia, was closely related to the idea of human motivation, for it has conveyed goal-directed motives, indicative of purposive behaviour that prevails as long as the goal is attained. Long until the late 1970s had nostalgia been overlooked by scholars, unbeknownst of the semantic substance behind the Greek roots constructing the word. The academia is indebted to Davis[95] that the term 'nostalgia' has been reintroduced, leaving aside its medical prejudices. As a result, his precursory work opened new possibilities for strengthening marketing efforts, cementing consumer loyalty, and so, generating higher purchase volumes.

The analysis of the international and national literature allowed to delve into nostalgia-oriented marketing endeavours with a proven record of reliability as adopted in the branding context. For sure, nostalgia was elected as the strategic means of reaching customers thanks to the incredible opportunities of television and the concurrent emergence of pop culture, thus attracting the attention of researchers in the fields of marketing and consumer behaviour. What is already known about the retrospective phenomenon is based upon observational studies that investigated customer needs, wants, attitudes, and opinions. The literature emphasises the widespread popularity of television as the main avenue to stimulating nostalgic references, having acknowledged that the content of these studies focused on nostalgic advertising as aired on TV or being printed in a magazine.[96] These findings provide some implications for foundational guidelines concerning marketing actions since the most effective way to accelerate nostalgia is by employing visual representations that significantly affect sight, considering the perceptual-cognitive nature of consumer behaviour.

Notes

1 Anspach, "Medical Dissertation on Nostalgia by Johannes Hofer, 1688", 376–391.
2 Lubiński, "The Study of Nostalgia-Oriented Strategy Aimed at Millennials on the Example of the LEGO Group", 86.
3 Holbrook and Schindler, "Echoes of the Dear Departed Past: Some Work in Progress on Nostalgia", 330.
4 Meltzer, *Euripides and the Poetics of Nostalgia*, 33.
5 McCann, "Nostalgia: A Review of the Literature", 165–182.
6 Starobinski, "The Idea of Nostalgia", 81–103.
7 Anspach, "Medical Dissertation on Nostalgia by Johannes Hofer, 1688", 376–391.
8 Havlena and Holak, "The Good Old Days: Observations on Nostalgia and Its Role in Consumer Behavior", 323–329.
9 Martin, "Nostalgia", 93–104.
10 McCann, "Nostalgia: A Review of the Literature", 165–182.
11 Zwingmann, "'Heimweh' or Nostalgic Reaction: A Conceptual Analysis and Interpretation of a Medico-Psychological Phenomenon", 3849–3850.
12 Guthrie, *Functional Nervous Disorders in Childhood*, 50–63.
13 McCann, "Nostalgia: A Review of the Literature", 165–182.
14 Hall, "A Study of Fears", 147–249.
15 Szasz, *The Myth of Mental Illness: Foundations of a Theory of Personal Conduct*, 8–15.
16 Conklin, *Principles of Adolescent Psychology*, 209–216.
17 McCann, "Nostalgia: A Descriptive and Comparative Study", 97–104.
18 Prete, "L'assedio della lontananza", 17.
19 Davis, *Yearning for Yesterday: A Sociology of Nostalgia*, 4.
20 Matt, "You Can't Go Home Again: Homesickness and Nostalgia in U.S. History", 469–497.
21 Kaplan, "The Psychopathology of Nostalgia", 466.
22 Peters, "Reflections on the Origin and Aim of Nostalgia", 135–136.
23 Nawas and Platt, "A Future Oriented Theory of Nostalgia", 51–54.

24 Fodor, "Varieties of Nostalgia", 25–38.
25 Martin, "Nostalgia", 102.
26 Rose, "The Homes of Homesick Girls", 181–189.
27 Lippert, "Über Heimweh", 83.
28 Nawas and Platt, "A Future Oriented Theory of Nostalgia", 51–56.
29 Darwin, *The Expression of the Emotions in Man and Animals*, 216.
30 Werman, "Normal and Pathological Nostalgia", 387–398.
31 Kaplan, "The Psychopathology of Nostalgia", 466–486.
32 Batcho, "Personal Nostalgia, World View, Memory, and Emotionality", 411–432.
33 Routledge, *Nostalgia: A Psychological Resource*, 6.
34 Taylor and Konrad, "Scaling Dispositions Toward the Past", 290.
35 Davis, *Yearning for Yesterday: A Sociology of Nostalgia*, 8–9.
36 Davis, *Yearning for Yesterday: A Sociology of Nostalgia*, 17–28.
37 Wildschut et al., "Nostalgia: Content, Triggers, Functions", 975–993.
38 Sedikides et al., "Nostalgia: Past, Present, and Future", 304–307; Wildschut et al., "Nostalgia: Content, Triggers, Functions", 981; Kaplan, "The Psychopathology of Nostalgia", 466.
39 Wildschut et al., "Nostalgia: Content, Triggers, Functions", 981; Peters, "Reflections on the Origin and Aim of Nostalgia", 145; Werman, "Normal and Pathological Nostalgia", 387–398.
40 Baker and Kennedy, "Death by Nostalgia: A Diagnosis of Context-Specific Cases", 169; Belk, "The Role of Possessions in Constructing and Maintaining a Sense of Past", 670; Stern, "Historical and Personal Nostalgia in Advertising Text: The Fin de Siècle Effect", 11–22; Wildschut et al., "Nostalgia as a Repository of Social Connectedness: The Role of Attachment-Related Avoidance", 573.
41 Batcho, "Nostalgia: A Psychological Perspective", 141; Peters, "Reflections on the Origin and Aim of Nostalgia", 136; Werman, "Normal and Pathological Nostalgia", 388; Wildschut et al., "Nostalgia: Content, Triggers, Functions", 975–983.
42 Holbrook and Schindler, "Echoes of the Dear Departed Past: Some Work in Progress on Nostalgia", 330.
43 Havlena and Holak, "The Good Old Days: Observations on Nostalgia and Its Role in Consumer Behavior", 323–329.
44 Stern, "Historical and Personal Nostalgia in Advertising Text: The Fin de Siècle Effect", 11–22.
45 Holbrook and Schindler, "Nostalgic Bonding: Exploring the Role of Nostalgia in the Consumption Experience", 107–127.
46 Holbrook and Schindler, "Echoes of the Dear Departed Past: Some Work in Progress on Nostalgia", 331.
47 Belk, "Possessions and the Sense of Past", 114–115.
48 Pickering and Keightley, "The Modalities of Nostalgia", 920.
49 Boym, *The Future of Nostalgia*, 75.
50 Holak and Havlena, "Feelings, Fantasies, and Memories: An Examination of the Emotional Components of Nostalgia", 218.
51 Holbrook and Schindler, "Echoes of the Dear Departed Past: Some Work in Progress on Nostalgia", 330.

52 Havlena and Holak, "The Good Old Days: Observations on Nostalgia and Its Role in Consumer Behavior", 323–329.
53 Stern, "Historical and Personal Nostalgia in Advertising Text: The Fin de Siècle Effect", 11–22.
54 Baker and Kennedy, "Death by Nostalgia: A Diagnosis of Context-Specific Cases", 169–174.
55 Rousseau and Venter, "The Relationship Between Nostalgia and Consumer Preference: Replication and Extension", 32–36.
56 Goulding, "Romancing the Past: Heritage Visiting and the Nostalgic Customer", 565–592.
57 Pascal et al., "The Influence of Evoked Nostalgia on Consumers' Responses to Advertising: An Exploratory Study", 39–47.
58 Brown et al., "Teaching Old Brands New Tricks: Retro Branding and the Revival of Brand Meaning", 19–33; Prieto and Boistel, "Rétromarketing dans l'automobile. La stratégie 'anti-rétro' de Citroën DS", 31–49.
59 Turner, "A Note on Nostalgia", 147–156.
60 Leigh et al., "The Consumer Quest for Authenticity: The Multiplicity of Meanings Within the MG Subculture of Consumption", 481–493.
61 Belk, "Possessions and the Extended Self", 139.
62 Kleine et al., "How Is a Possession 'Me' or 'Not Me'? Characterizing Types and an Antecedent of Material Possession Attachment", 341.
63 Stern, "Historical and Personal Nostalgia in Advertising Text: The Fin de Siècle Effect", 11–22.
64 Holbrook and Schindler, "Market Segmentation Based on Age and Attitude Toward the Past: Concepts, Methods, and Findings Concerning Nostalgic Influences on Customer Tastes", 27–30.
65 Goulding, "Romancing the Past: Heritage Visiting and the Nostalgic Customer", 565–570.
66 Rindfleisch and Sprott, "Moving Forward on Looking Backward: Advancing Theory and Practice in Nostalgia", 34; Sierra and McQuitty, "Attitudes and Emotions as Determinants of Nostalgia Purchases: An Application of Social Identity Theory", 99; Stern, "Historical and Personal Nostalgia in Advertising Text: The Fin de Siècle Effect", 18.
67 Stern, "Historical and Personal Nostalgia in Advertising Text: The Fin de Siècle Effect", 11–22.
68 Belk, "The Role of Possessions in Constructing and Maintaining a Sense of Past", 669–676.
69 Emmons, "Striving for the Sacred: Personal Goals, Life Meaning, and Religion", 732–733.
70 Beverland and Farrelly, "The Quest for Authenticity in Consumption: Consumers' Purposive Choice of Authentic Cues to Shape Experienced Outcomes", 839.
71 Belk et al., "The Fire of Desire: A Multi-Sited Inquiry Into Consumer Passion", 342.
72 Belk et al., "The Fire of Desire: A Multi-Sited Inquiry Into Consumer Passion", 341.
73 Higson, "Nostalgia Is Not What It Used to Be: Heritage Films, Nostalgia Web-Sites, and Contemporary Consumers", 120–132.

74 Belk, "Possessions and the Sense of Past", 128.
75 Davis, *Yearning for Yesterday: A Sociology of Nostalgia*, 222.
76 Brown et al., "Teaching Old Brands New Tricks: Retro Branding and the Revival of Brand Meaning", 19–30.
77 Kao, "An Exploratory Study of Collective Nostalgia", 514.
78 Boym, *The Future of Nostalgia*, 79–80.
79 Stern, "Historical and Personal Nostalgia in Advertising Text: The Fin de Siècle Effect", 13.
80 Kessous and Roux, "A Semiotic Analysis of Nostalgia as a Connection to the Past", 192–198.
81 Grębosz-Krawczyk and Siuda, "Identification of Nostalgic Brands Existing on the Polish Market in the Light of Empirical Research", 59.
82 Baker and Kennedy, "Death by Nostalgia: A Diagnosis of Context-Specific Cases", 169–174.
83 Alba and Hutchinson, "Dimensions of Consumer Expertise", 429.
84 Boym, *The Future of Nostalgia*, 79–80.
85 Baker and Kennedy, "Death by Nostalgia: A Diagnosis of Context-Specific Cases", 169–174.
86 Hamilton and Wagner, "Commercialised Nostalgia: Staging Consumer Experiences in Small Businesses", 816.
87 Davis, *Yearning for Yesterday: A Sociology of Nostalgia*, 122–123.
88 Baker and Kennedy, "Death by Nostalgia: A Diagnosis of Context-Specific Cases", 169–174.
89 Higson, "Nostalgia Is Not What It Used to Be: Heritage Films, Nostalgia Web-Sites, and Contemporary Consumers", 121.
90 Routledge, *Nostalgia: A Psychological Resource*, 114–115.
91 Davis, *Yearning for Yesterday: A Sociology of Nostalgia*, 415.
92 Wilson, *Nostalgia: Sanctuary of Meaning*, 7.
93 Pickering and Keightley, "The Modalities of Nostalgia", 930.
94 Davis, *Yearning for Yesterday: A Sociology of Nostalgia*, 415.
95 Davis, *Yearning for Yesterday: A Sociology of Nostalgia*, 415.
96 Havlena and Holak, "Exploring Nostalgia Imagery Through the Use of Consumer Collages", 35–42.

Reference list

Alba, Joseph W., and J. Wesley Hutchinson. "Dimensions of Consumer Expertise." *Journal of Consumer Research* 13, no. 1 (1987): 411–454.

Anspach, Carolyn Kiser. "Medical Dissertation on Nostalgia by Johannes Hofer, 1688." *Bulletin of the Institute of the History of Medicine* 2, no. 6 (1934): 376–391.

Baker, Stacey Menzel., and Patrizia Kennedy. "Death by Nostalgia: A Diagnosis of Context-Specific Cases." *Advances in Consumer Research* 21 (1994): 169–174.

Batcho, Krystine I. "Nostalgia: A Psychological Perspective." *Perceptual and Motor Skills* 80, no. 1 (1995): 131–143. https://doi.org/10.2466/pms.1995.80.1.131.

Batcho, Krystine I. “Personal Nostalgia, World View, Memory, and Emotionality.” *Perceptual and Motor Skills* 87, no. 2 (1998): 411–432. https://doi.org/10.2466/pms.1998.87.2.411.
Belk, Russell W. “Possessions and the Extended Self.” *Journal of Consumer Research* 15, no. 2 (1988): 139–168.
Belk, Russell W. “The Role of Possessions in Constructing and Maintaining a Sense of Past.” *Advances in Consumer Research* 17 (1990): 669–676.
Belk, Russell W. “Possessions and the Sense of Past.” *Odyssey* (1991): 114–115.
Belk, Russell W., Güliz Ger, and Søren Askegaard. “The Fire of Desire: A Multi-Sited Inquiry Into Consumer Passion.” *Journal of Consumer Research* 30, no. 3 (2003): 326–351.
Beverland, Michael B., and Francis J. Farrelly. “The Quest for Authenticity in Consumption: Consumers’ Purposive Choice of Authentic Cues to Shape Experienced Outcomes.” *Journal of Consumer Research* 36, no. 5 (2010): 838–856.
Boym, Svetlana. *The Future of Nostalgia*. New York: Basic Books, 2001.
Brown, Stephen, Robert Kozinets, and John Sherry. “Teaching Old Brands New Tricks: Retro Branding and the Revival of Brand Meaning.” *Journal of Marketing* 67 (2003): 19–33.
Conklin, Edwin S. *Principles of Adolescent Psychology*. New York: Henry Holt and Company, 1935.
Darwin, Charles. *The Expression of the Emotions in Man and Animals*. 2nd ed. Cambridge University Press, 2009.
Davis, Fred. *Yearning for Yesterday: A Sociology of Nostalgia*. New York: The Free Press, 1979.
Emmons, Robert A. “Striving for the Sacred: Personal Goals, Life Meaning, and Religion.” *Journal of Social Issues* 61, no. 4 (2005): 732–733.
Fodor, Nandor. “Varieties of Nostalgia.” *Psychoanalytic Review* 37 (1950): 25–38.
Goulding, Christina. “Romancing the Past: Heritage Visiting and the Nostalgic Customer.” *Psychology and Marketing* 18 (2001): 565–592.
Grębosz-Krawczyk, Magdalena, and Dagna Siuda. “Identification of Nostalgic Brands Existing on the Polish Market in the Light of Empirical Research.” *Studia Ekonomiczne. Zeszyty Naukowe Uniwersytetu Ekonomicznego w Katowicach* 330 (2017): 57–65.
Guthrie, Leonard. *Functional Nervous Disorders in Childhood*. London: Oxford University Press, 1907.
Hall, G. Stanley. “A Study of Fears.” *The American Journal of Psychology* 8, no. 2 (1897): 147–249. https://doi.org/10.2307/1410940.
Hamilton, Kathy A., and Beverly Wagner. “Commercialised Nostalgia: Staging Consumer Experiences in Small Businesses.” *European Journal of Marketing* 48, no. 5/6 (2014): 813–832.
Havlena, William J., and Susan L. Holak. “The Good Old Days: Observations on Nostalgia and Its Role in Consumer Behavior.” *Advances in Consumer Research* 18 (1991): 323–329.
Havlena, William J., and Susan L. Holak. “Exploring Nostalgia Imagery Through the Use of Consumer Collages.” *Advances in Consumer Research* 23 (1996): 35–42.

Higson, Andrew. "Nostalgia Is Not What It Used to Be: Heritage Films, Nostalgia Web-Sites, and Contemporary Consumers." *Consumption Markets & Culture* 17, no. 2 (2014): 120–142. https://doi.org/10.1080/10253866.2013.776305.

Holak, Susan L., and William J. Havlena. "Feelings, Fantasies, and Memories: An Examination of the Emotional Components of Nostalgia." *Journal of Business Research* 42, no. 3 (1998): 217–226. https://doi.org/10.1016/S0148-2963(97)00119-7.

Holbrook, Morris B., and Robert M. Schindler. "Echoes of the Dear Departed Past: Some Work in Progress on Nostalgia." *Advances in Consumer Research* 18 (1991): 330–333.

Holbrook, Morris B., and Robert M. Schindler. "Market Segmentation Based on Age and Attitude Toward the Past: Concepts, Methods, and Findings Concerning Nostalgic Influences on Customer Tastes." *Journal of Business Research* 37, no. 1 (1996): 27–39.

Holbrook, Morris B., and Robert M. Schindler. "Nostalgic Bonding: Exploring the Role of Nostalgia in the Consumption Experience." *Journal of Consumer Behavior* 3, no. 2 (2003): 107–127. https://doi.org/10.1002/cb.127.

Kao, Faye. "An Exploratory Study of Collective Nostalgia." *Advances in Consumer Research* 40 (2012): 514–518.

Kaplan, Harvey A. "The Psychopathology of Nostalgia." *Psychoanalytic Review* 74, no. 4 (1987): 465–486.

Kessous, Aurélie, and Elyette Roux. "A Semiotic Analysis of Nostalgia as a Connection to the Past." *Qualitative Market Research: An International Journal* 11, no. 2 (2008): 192–212.

Kleine, Susan S., Robert E. Kleine, and Chris T. Allen. "How Is a Possession 'Me' or 'Not Me'? Characterizing Types and an Antecedent of Material Possession Attachment." *Journal of Consumer Research* 22, no. 3 (1995): 327–343.

Leigh, Thomas W., Cara Peters, and Jeremy Shelton. "The Consumer Quest for Authenticity: The Multiplicity of Meanings Within the MG Subculture of Consumption." *Journal of the Academy of Marketing Science* 34, no. 4 (2006): 481–493.

Lippert, E. "*Über Heimweh*." *Zeitschrift für Kinderpsychiatrie* 17 (1950): 79–84.

Lubiński, Kamil. "The Study of Nostalgia-Oriented Strategy Aimed at Millennials on the Example of the LEGO Group." *Journal of Intercultural Management* 12, no. 2 (2020): 86–105. https://doi.org/10.2478/joim-2020-0039.

Martin, Alexander R. "Nostalgia." *The American Journal of Psychoanalysis* 14, no. 1 (1954): 93–104. https://doi.org/10.1007/BF01872229.

Matt, Susan J. "You Can't Go Home Again: Homesickness and Nostalgia in U.S. History." *Journal of American History* 94, no. 2 (2007): 469–497. https://doi.org/10.2307/25094961.

McCann, W. H. "Nostalgia: A Review of the Literature." *Psychological Bulletin* 38, no. 3 (1941): 165–182. https://doi.org/10.1037/h0057354.

McCann, W. H. "Nostalgia: A Descriptive and Comparative Study." *Journal of Genetic Psychology* 62 (1943): 97–104.

Meltzer, Gary S. *Euripides and the Poetics of Nostalgia*. Cambridge: Cambridge University Press, 2006.

Nawas, M. Mike, and Jerome J. Platt. "A Future Oriented Theory of Nostalgia." *Journal of Individual Psychology* 21 (1965): 51–57.

Pascal, Vincent, David E. Sprott, and Darrel D. Muehling. "The Influence of Evoked Nostalgia on Consumers' Responses to Advertising: An Exploratory Study." *Journal of Current Issues and Research in Advertising* 24, no. 1 (2002): 39–47.

Peters, Roderick. "Reflections on the Origin and Aim of Nostalgia." *Journal of Analytical Psychology* 30, no. 2 (1985): 135–148. https://doi.org/10.1111/j.1465-5922.1985.00135.x.

Pickering, Michael, and Emily Keightley. "The Modalities of Nostalgia." *Current Sociology* 54, no. 6 (2006): 919–941. https://doi.org/10.1177/0011392106068458.

Prete, Antonio. "L'assedio della lontananza." In *Nostalgia: Storia di un Sentimento*, edited by Antonio Prete, 3–22. Milan: Raffaello Cortina, 2018.

Prieto, Marc, and Philippe Boistel. "Rétromarketing dans l'automobile. La stratégie "anti-rétro" de Citroën DS." *Revue Française de Gestion* 239 (2014): 31–49.

Rindfleisch, Aric, and David E. Sprott. "Moving Forward on Looking Backward: Advancing Theory and Practice in Nostalgia." *Advances in Consumer Research* 27 (2000): 34–35.

Rose, A. A. "The Homes of Homesick Girls." *Journal of Child Psychiatry* 1 (1948): 181–189.

Rousseau, Gabriel G., and Danie J. L. Venter. "The Relationship Between Nostalgia and Consumer Preference: Replication and Extension." *Journal of Industrial Psychology* 26, no. 2 (2000): 32–36.

Routledge, Clay. *Nostalgia: A Psychological Resource*. New York: Routledge, 2016.

Sedikides, Constantine, Tim Wildschut, Jamie Arndt, and Clay Routledge. "Nostalgia: Past, Present, and Future." *Current Directions in Psychological Science* 17, no. 5 (2008): 304–307. https://doi.org/10.1111/j.1467-8721.2008.00595.x.

Sierra, Jeremy J., and Shaun McQuitty. "Attitudes and Emotions as Determinants of Nostalgia Purchases: An Application of Social Identity Theory." *Journal of Marketing Theory and Practice* 15, no. 2 (2007): 99–112. https://doi.org/10.2753/MTP1069-6679150201.

Starobinski, Jean. "The Idea of Nostalgia." *Diogenes* 14, no. 54 (1966): 81–103. https://doi.org/10.1177/039219216601405405.

Stern, Barbara B. "Historical and Personal Nostalgia in Advertising Text: The Fin de Siècle Effect." *Journal of Advertising* 21, no. 4 (1992): 11–22.

Szasz, Thomas. *The Myth of Mental Illness: Foundations of a Theory of Personal Conduct*. Harper Perrenial, 2010.

Taylor, S. Martin, and Victor A. Konrad. "Scaling Dispositions Toward the Past." *Environment and Behavior* 12, no. 3 (1980): 283–307. https://doi.org/10.1177/0013916580123001.

Turner, Bryan. "A Note on Nostalgia." *Theory, Culture & Society* 4 (1987): 147–156.

Werman, David S. "Normal and Pathological Nostalgia." *Journal of the American Psychoanalytic Association* 25, no. 2 (1977): 387–398. https://doi.org/10.1177/000306517702500205.

Wildschut, Tim, Constantine Sedikides, Clay Routledge, Jamie Arndt, and Federico Cordaro. "Nostalgia as a Repository of Social Connectedness: The Role of Attachment-Related Avoidance." *Journal of Personality and Social Psychology* 98, no. 4 (2010): 573–586. https://doi.org/10.1037/a0017597.

Wildschut, Tim, Constantine Sedikides, Jamie Arndt, and Clay Routledge. "Nostalgia: Content, Triggers, Functions." *Journal of Personality and Social Psychology* 91, no. 5 (2006): 975–993. https://doi.org/10.1037/0022-3514.91.5.975.

Wilson, Janelle L. *Nostalgia* (2014)*: Sanctuary of Meaning*. University Digital Conservancy. https://hdl.handle.net/11299/189216.

Zwingmann, Charles A. A. " 'Heimweh' or Nostalgic Reaction: A Conceptual Analysis and Interpretation of a Medico-Psychological Phenomenon." *Dissertation Abstracts* 2 (1960): 3849–3850.

2 Nostalgic branding

2.1 Definitions and types of Nostalgic brand

A nostalgic brand is one associated with a past – whether personal or historical, recent or distant. It can also be seen as a brand positioning strategy aimed at fostering a more favourable perception of the brand and increasing purchase likelihood by creating associations with the past.[1] According to the definition by Holbrook and Schindler,[2] such a brand should evoke memories of a time when the consumer was younger. While Aaker[3] conceptualised brand identity as active and forward-looking, brand image is often passive and tied to the past, which explains the widespread use of nostalgia in contemporary marketing. Two types of nostalgic brands can be distinguished[4]:

- Generational brands – based on a real nostalgia (relating to the own direct and personal memories), having the individual or collective character.
- Transgenerational brands – based on real nostalgia or a simulated nostalgia (referring indirectly to the individual experiences and memories of other people, as well as to the collective experiences and memories when affected by historical nostalgia) having the individual or collective character.

It is believed that generational brands are based on Stern's long-standing nostalgia, whereas transgenerational brands derive from the concept of first-time nostalgia.

When adapting a nostalgia-imbued approach, the first to be introduced ought to be the company's core customers, for it is they who shall express their devotion to the brand by answering to the nostalgic message. As people who had been a part of a company's history, core customers unconsciously set nostalgic trends by purchasing these products that satisfied their expectations. Only then may a company attempt to use this method to address new consumers. To enhance its nostalgic brand image, the brand must follow a path it had once started, thereby maintaining its primary discourse. At the same time, it must be assured that the nostalgic values a company is conjuring up have to be diversified enough such that they are accepted by a wider audience,

DOI: 10.4324/9781003606079-4

including the brand's primary consumers. Brand managers, therefore, should seek such values that appeal to their consumers and simultaneously provide the much-desired differential effect. In turn, these retrospective values will serve as a basis for further brand positioning and the development of a promotional campaign.[5]

Given the ability to create a mediated illusion of a past period that once was, advertisers have come to realise that by giving their brands a sense of authenticity, an additional outcome will be achieved: not only will the target audience respond, but also other generations, thereby forging a generational link. Known as 'backward innovation', this technique has helped various companies relaunch and revive themselves, helping them survive and even flourish.[6] The products did not have to be the same as they had been – that would be too immense a task. It was the brand's heritage that allowed it to succeed.[7] The key was in encapsulating a seeming paradox, a combination of old and new. A company had to have existed in consumers' minds at some point in the past, yet another thing to consider was to make consumers perceive the brand as positively appealing.[8] And that is what advertisers have aspired to deliver through broadcasting TV commercials. When the target audience experiences turmoil, their need for safety and order enhances. As Holbrook[9] has noted, turning the past into a new desirable object in both the consumer products and communication channels is a promising area of marketing for nostalgia.

The aim of positioning based on nostalgia is to provide the consumer with stimuli by evoking familiar events from the past. The positioning of a nostalgic brand should be based on its history, values, identity, and positioning in the past.[10] All elements of brand identity, such as brand physicality, brand personality expressed through its value system, brand culture, brand reflection, relationships with target customers, and brand self-image, should be analysed in detail. The key to successful positioning of a nostalgic brand is understanding how to effectively refer to the past, arousing positive emotions of consumers.

On the basis of the historical background of the brand and the target audience, the brand should be classified as generational or transgenerational. This choice is crucial to the positioning of a nostalgic brand. Transgenerational brands can use all kinds of nostalgia, referring both to the consumer's own past and to a past that the consumer has not experienced. In the case of generational brands, there is an appeal to personal and collective nostalgia by referring to the direct experiences of the consumer. Any nostalgic brand should target a specific segment of the population: its target core. The main goal of a nostalgic brand is the audience that most identifies with its values. Such consumers are by definition more sensitive and therefore more loyal to the brand's values. The nostalgic brand should be directed to this target core; it is these consumers who will intuitively express their attachment and establish relationships with the nostalgic brand. To solidify its nostalgic image, the brand must continue its original discourse, emphasising the relationship with the original purpose. At the same time, make sure that its nostalgic values are universal enough to be accepted by a wider audience, including all consumers for whom the brand's products are intended.

Brand managers need to find the most important nostalgic values that consumers expect and which – at the same time – distinguish the brand from competitors. It is these values that will be the basis for positioning and creating a promotional campaign. The identity of nostalgic brands is based primarily on positive memories of consumers. Brands managed in accordance with the philosophy of nostalgia marketing are based on a characteristic semiotics expressed in nostalgic storytelling, symbolic narration, and metaphor of the message. The choice of final brand positioning allows reaching the chosen goal by creating a clear, precise, and unique nostalgic image in the mind of the target consumer.

According to Grębosz-Krawczyk,[11] the concept of nostalgic brand positioning should be distinguished from the positioning of a nostalgic brand. Nostalgic brand positioning is a brand positioning strategy that aims to have a positive impact on the individual by creating associations with the past (not necessarily related to a specific brand or branded product). Research has shown that marketing activities can arouse artificial nostalgia in consumers,[12] and practical examples show that even brands with a short history are able to emphasise certain historical events preceding the birth of a brand.

On the other hand, the positioning of a nostalgic brand is expressed through the implementation of a brand positioning strategy aimed at highlighting the historical roots of the brand, which can play a significant role in the consumer's decision-making process by evoking positive emotions of a nostalgic nature. Consequently, the positioning of a nostalgic brand applies to nostalgic brands, and nostalgic brand positioning can be used for both nostalgic and non-nostalgic brands.

2.2 Nostalgia in research on consumer behaviour and brand management

Although, as already been covered, studying nostalgia is not relatively new, its latest preoccupation with the disciplines of marketing and consumer behaviour is. Routledge[13] believes that especially those were the invaluable contributions of consumer research that shed light on the underestimated power of nostalgia and thus seeded a new array of publications. Researchers found that nostalgia in this regard is a matter of preference or taste that had been developing when people were in their early adolescence and formed when they reached late adolescence.[14] Perhaps the first research to have started the so-called new wave of the research on nostalgia was the exploratory study by Holbrook and Schindler[15] in which they investigated the development of musical tastes in the context of the nostalgic feeling. Participants varying in age from 16 to 86 were asked to rank the excerpts of the popular songs (but not charted inside the top three) they had heard from a tape player. The results indicated that the subjects preferred those songs that were first released when they were younger. The researchers were also able to determine the approximate age at which participants were first introduced to a song of their preference, which in this case was 23.5 years old. Given the account that people prefer music that was popular back in the times of their youth, a conclusion was made that music from a personally lived past may lead to nostalgic feelings.

Without a doubt, the scholars must have been aware of the fact that nostalgia is way deeper than that. The findings suggested, at least in the case of the music, that by the age of 24, people form an ultimate set of preferences towards particular products of choice. The authors have suggested the external factors, like the pressure exerted by the peer groups, to be the case. Moreover, they have admitted that exposure to stimuli that reminded people of things from the times of their youth could influence them to the consumption associated with those things. However, it demanded a broader perspective and far more representative samples. In an attempt to further clarify this still-exploratory phenomenon, Holbrook[16] developed a nostalgia index scale to assess the nostalgia proneness among movie viewers. He conducted two simultaneous studies to determine whether or not age and proneness are two independent elements of a nostalgic consumption. The first study used the same sample from the previous research made by Holbrook and Schindler.[17] The second study focused on a wide range of age inclusiveness among the participants. Respondents were given a list of each film that won the Academy Award in the Best Picture category until the moment when the research was conducted (1993). On the basis of the conceptual contribution by Davis in the late 1970s, Holbrook[18] managed to create a set of 20 items in the form of universal statements designed to investigate the nostalgic proneness. The results were consistent with those of the previous study, confirming that preference towards maudlin objects is being shaped until late adolescence, but more importantly, it showed that age and proneness are two separate factors of nostalgic consumption in the context of movies.

As if that were not enough, Holbrook and Schindler,[19] still aware of the caveats and uncertainties surrounding their scholarship, have advanced their research to see how the results would change in case of the consumption of cultural products. In their next study, the authors replicated the method of preceding studies concerning the development of preferences during a significant moment of life (generally late adolescence). This time, they sought to determine if this age-based phenomenon does occur in the case of cultural products usually presented in the form of visual representations of movie stars and if there exists a notable difference between how males and females are inclined to such imagery in terms of nostalgia proneness. The results confirmed that as for aesthetic preferences, nostalgia indeed influences consumer choice.

Furthermore, male respondents were way more likely to elicit nostalgic feelings, primarily towards the images portraying female movie stars, than female respondents in the analogous scenario.

The fundamental principle of the phenomenon discovered by Holbrook and Schindler was that sensory experience linked to positive decoding of the nostalgic message contained in an advert sparked both the affection towards the brand and the purchasing intention of products marketed by this brand.[20] Holak and Havlena[21] identified two varieties of such strategies adapted by the companies: the first focuses on offering an authentic product originated or manufactured somewhere in the past period, and the second, using an illusion of the good old times to promote a brand new product. As has been previously noted hereinabove, these two have been identified by Stern[22] as 'historical' and 'personal' nostalgia. Although it has not been firmly established which approach would be of better use for a company, Stern argued that using personal nostalgia helps a consumer rebuild his self-concept distorted by an episode of an unhappy childhood, whereas the use of historical nostalgia seems fair with offerings connected with social statuses, as apparent in the automotive industry. At this point, it should be acknowledged that Holbrook and Schindler[23] also observed that males are peculiarly disposed to feel nostalgic for automobiles from their youth.

Moving back to Holak and Havlena,[24] their 1992 study endeavoured to test if special occasions (such as birthdays, holidays, and reunions) may trigger nostalgia. The methodology was replicated from their much earlier investigation concentrating on emotional components of the purchase behaviour. Once introduced to a brief definition of nostalgia, respondents were asked to describe their personal nostalgic feelings in the context of a person, an object, and a unique event. The results confirmed that special occasions are typically identified as time periods when positive nostalgia is experienced. Moreover, there was a visible connection between people, objects, and events, thereby unfolding themes of nostalgic experiences. The authors had earlier reported that those themes have been appearing more commonly in commercials as part of a nostalgia-based marketing strategy.[25] As a result, the experience of watching such an advertisement that brings to mind those unique events of tremendous value can provoke nostalgic feelings.

These developments were extended for the purposes of the authors' other study[26] examining the emotional elements surrounding nostalgia. It has been done by replicating the methodology and using the exact sample from the 1992 research. Thus, the results were relying heavily upon the set of detailed descriptions regarding nostalgic experience in three contexts. The study featured an expert rating of emotions done by behavioural specialists using a set of scales designed to measure the content of emotions so that each of the 62 participants was treated individually. Each expert was asked to evaluate the emotive dimension of the provided account of nostalgic feelings using either the 18-item PAD index or the more complex 40-item standardised emotional profile index. The idea was to obtain the bittersweet image of nostalgia as depicted in the literature, whereas those warm and positive feelings would be more evident since they were believed to be of greater importance to advertisers. Results supported the prediction that the positive emotions of gratitude, warmth, and joy take part in the nostalgic process of reminiscing. However, it was also found that these positive emotions were often intertwined with sadness and the desire to change that experience, which not only marked the presence of the bittersweet trait but also confirmed it to be true.

In both studies, Holak and Havlena[27] confirmed that, all things considered, nostalgia is a multi-layered phenomenon that is difficult to predict its effect on people, given its ability to cast both positive and negative emotions. Routledge argues that despite such a meticulous approach as taken by the authors for investigating nostalgia, it lacked values of qualitative research.[28]

To test the assertion that advertising-evoked nostalgia affects the consumers' attitude towards the advertised brand and increases the likelihood of purchasing from that brand, Pascal, Sprott, and Muehling[29] conducted preliminary research in which they developed the evoked nostalgia scale. The authors prepared a set of black-and-white printed adverts of brands believed to be unknown to the subjects. Participants were then instructed to evaluate only the two of them, particularly the second and the fifth advert. Little did the participants know that these two were, in fact, the experimental stimuli of the research. Two brands have been chosen by the authors for the purposes of that study: Toshiba and Kodak. The researchers used the printed advertisements of the products referring to both the photography (Kodak film) and motion pictures (Toshiba DVD player) as a practical follow-up to the findings of Holbrook and Schindler concerning the consumption of cultural products. The results were consistent with the authors' starting assertion. It was shown that the ad-evoked nostalgia significantly increased the likelihood of purchase of the Kodak product and slightly increased for Toshiba. Moreover, it was only the attitude towards the advertised brand rather than the advertisement itself that was affecting the possibility of purchase behaviour. One limitation of this particular study, however, was that all the responses were collected from undergraduate university students.

Much more pertinently perhaps, the propensity of an individual to be nostalgic in the context of print advertising has been investigated in more detail by Reisenwitz, Iyer, and Cutler.[30] The scholars have asserted that there must be a correlation between nostalgia proneness and its intensity (hereby understood as the strength of an individual's wistfulness)[31] towards such stimuli. In order to test this assumption, the authors juxtaposed nostalgic advertisements with contemporary non-nostalgic ones. It is worth noting that it was the first time when the study no longer focused on cultural products, as has happened with the previous studies on the subject (e.g., Holbrook and Schindler, 1994[32]; Pascal et al., 2002).[33] Instead, the participants were shown advertisements for food (cookies and mineral water) and household cleaning products (bathroom cleaner, window cleaner). The procedure was designed such that the participants were to determine which of the advertised products they would prefer if they had to make a purchase decision. The participants were then instructed to complete a short questionnaire so that the authors would evaluate nostalgia intensity using a 12-item scale developed by Baker and Kennedy.[34] However, only those participants aged 24 and older were included for the final study, considering the already established evidence whereby nostalgic preference develops by the age of 24 years. The results confirmed that an individual's nostalgia proneness is undoubtedly related to both nostalgia intensity towards the advertisement and the advertised brand.

However, the fact that research lent credibility to the widespread use of nostalgia-based advertising, and that individuals exhibited enthusiastic preferences for such offerings, did not imply that the cognitive factors driving these decisions were ever identified. In their first approach on the subject of nostalgia, Sierra and McQuitty[35] prepared a work-in-progress study with the use of the relatively unknown concept of Social Identity Theory (SIT) to better understand the reason why the consumers are particularly inclined to nostalgic purchases. To assess this, the authors first asked the respondents to indicate whether or not they did buy a nostalgic product. Having answered the question affirmatively, the respondents were then asked to specify a type of product they purchased. The most striking result to emerge from the data was that music, albeit intangible in its form unless the records like vinyl were considered to be 'music', was elected the most acquired nostalgic product. These findings, in this regard, paralleled the effects of the 1989 study by Holbrook and Schindler. Another important finding was that 'toys' scored high in this study as well, second to music.[36] Since toys are, no doubt, physical goods (e.g., action figures, wooden bricks, teddy bears), it follows, therefore, that the objects of the child's play are the most nostalgic tangible products on the market. After providing these exemplary purchases, participants responded to questions assessing their attitude towards the past period, which the product has represented. The results supported the proposal that SIT may prove critical in understanding the psychological mechanism of nostalgia. Nonetheless, this problem has received limited attention in literature.

There seemed to be an obvious, albeit banal, alignment between the effects of nostalgic advertisement and the individual's inherited attachment to the brand. In fact, however, this does not necessarily have to be true. Muehling, Sprott, and Sultan[37] tested whether or not past experience with a brand influences the emotional intensity towards nostalgic advertising. Specifically, the experimental stimuli they have used in their research were the print advertising of a popular toothpaste brand. Participants were selected in such a way that they must have been aware of the existence of the stimulus brand during their late adolescence or childhood (aged 35 and younger). First, the participants were asked to answer five questions indicating their previous experience with the brand. Second, the participants had to select only one statement that best described both their recent and preceding affection for that brand. Finally, the participants were presented printed advertisements in both nostalgic and non-nostalgic variants. It is also worth mentioning that these two variants were designed by the authors explicitly for the purpose of the research and have not been used by the toothpaste company anywhere before. After watching each printed material, the participants completed a questionnaire that was based on the one used in the 2002 study by Pascal et al.[38] Results were consistent with the authors' expectations. Previous experience with a brand, particularly during childhood, does influence both purchase intention and brand attitude; however, nostalgia advertising may stimulate as well those consumers who have not had such previous associations with the same brand before. Moreover, it was revealed that ad attitude and ad involvement appeared to be even stronger to non-devoted consumers.

The study by Grębosz-Krawczyk[39] represents, to date, the first documented attempt in Poland to address the issue of consumer attitudes and behaviour towards nostalgic brands in a systematic manner. Moreover, the study is the first to provide new empirical insights on the nostalgic phenomenon on a grand scale. In her monograph, the author formulated three main hypotheses concerning the measurement of the consumer-perceived brand equity of nostalgic brands, the consumers' affective reactions towards nostalgic brands, and the attitudes and behaviour of Polish consumers based on their demographics. The results represent new steps in expanding the still-growing stream of research by presenting the perspective of the post-communist countries, where access to globally branded products was limited, as opposed to Western countries unspoiled by the political-economic turmoil in a period between 1947 and 1989.

A pilot study was conducted on a sample of 100 respondents in the second quarter of 2017 with the aim of identifying the brands that evoke associations with the past. Then, the author[40] filtered out the brands that were not mentioned at least five times. This way, 24 nostalgic brands representing eight product categories were selected for the primary study. Because the study was concerned with measuring the levels of brand equity, the author also identified 24 non-nostalgic alternatives to the brands deemed as nostalgic. The final sample consisted of 1,000 participants representing Polish customers – following Aaker,[41] 'customer' underlines both the end users and the potential audience. The results of both the qualitative and quantitative studies showed that the brand equity of nostalgic brands is more robust than non-nostalgic ones. At this junction, it was found that Polish consumers react positively to nostalgic brands, regardless of the product's category. In short, there was no indication that living in a post-communist country would in any way jeopardise an individual's response to nostalgic brands. Likewise, the results provided partial support for the third hypothesis relating to the demographic characteristics of the respondents, with age being progressively related to nostalgic proneness; thus, the older the customer, the more likely that he recognises a nostalgic brand. Sex, however, was not found to be related to nostalgia, as indicated in earlier research attempts.[42] Overall, the findings of Grębosz-Krawczyk[43] provided a unique contribution to the research on nostalgia by first introducing the dual characterisation of nostalgic brands and corresponding positioning strategies, second by the analyses of consumers' attitudes and behaviour towards nostalgic brands, third by practical recommendations regarding the positioning of a nostalgic brand in the settings of the Polish market, and finally by the application of the expert's study.

Examples of previous investigations of nostalgia in the context of consumer behaviour are presented in Table 2.1.

Nostalgia, in conclusion, is widely used in marketing strategies, and as Kessous and Roux[44] have remarked, this has grown into an international phenomenon permeating every aspect of the marketing mix. According to Brown et al.,[45] many long-forgotten brands were either resurrected or relaunched after the adoption of this technique. Specifically, the scholars were able to establish that nostalgia used as stimuli in advertising messages does influence brand attitudes and purchase behaviour. A possible explanation for these observations may lie in the human's curiosity that makes them stop and pay more attention to food, such as a thirst for knowledge. As Unger[46] argues, as long as nostalgia is perceived to be novel, it shall give impetus to such curiosity. Much of the initial effort in the 1990s has devoted attention towards spontaneous purchase scenarios, thereby underestimating the power of nostalgia. Nevertheless, there remains one significant concern surrounding the notion. Namely, that despite all of what has been thus written on the subject, the literature lacks a specific answer regarding the motivations for nostalgic attitudes and behaviour.[47] So far, however, there has been little discussion about the use of nostalgia in the context of the consumers' motivations.

2.3 Nostalgia in the management of a brand in the toy industry

Consistent with the guidelines of systematic literature review methodology, the author assumed that the searching process would be based on strict inclusion criteria of the existing literature. First, the combination of the following keywords 'toys', 'nostalgia', 'nostalgic', and 'toy industry' was selected to find core articles that would address the theme of nostalgia within the toy industry. The choice of keywords in the English language seems justifiable given the account of studies written in the English language. Thus, there is a lack of studies dealing with texts written in other languages. As noted by Green (as cited in Czakon et al., 2019),[48] this may be considered a weakness of which the author is aware. However, as usual in papers in management disciplines, a particular keyword may be featured in a database as ancillary. Therefore, it was crucial to focus only on those articles whose keywords reflected a pertinent, not an ancillary, character of the research.

Table 2.1 Examples of previous studies of nostalgia in consumer behaviour

Author(s) and year	*Principal research question*	*Methodology*	*Findings*
Holbrook and Schindler (1989)	Do aesthetic tastes shape preferences towards popular music?	Quantitative (survey research)	Preferences towards popular music appear to reflect tastes acquired during late adolescence or early adulthood.
Holak and Havlena (1992)	Do special occasions have the capacity to trigger nostalgia?	Quantitative (survey research)	Special occasions are typically identified as time periods when positive nostalgia is experienced.
Holbrook (1993)	Are nostalgia proneness and age two separate components of nostalgic consumption?	Quantitative (survey research)	Nostalgic consumption differs depending on age and nostalgia proneness, which are two exclusive aspects of nostalgic preference patterns.
Holak and Havlena (1998)	Which types of emotions are elicited in nostalgic experiences?	Quantitative (survey research based on the respondents' descriptions of nostalgic feeling)	Nostalgia experiences can result in both positive and negative emotional responses.
Brown and Humphreys (2002)	Can nostalgia be used to understand how individual and organisational identity are developed?	Qualitative (interviews)	Through shared memories, nostalgia cultivates and maintains individual and group identity.
Pascal, Sprott, and Muehling (2002)	Do ads containing nostalgic cues positively influence consumers' responses to the ad?	Qualitative (projecting technique) and quantitative (survey research)	There is a positive relationship between print ads that create nostalgic reactions and attitudes about the ad and brand and purchase intentions of the advertised product.
Schindler and Holbrook (2003)	What are the effects of early experience on consumer preferences?	Qualitative (interviews)	A liking for the past can increase the likelihood that items people purchased as youths continue to be purchased when they are adults.

(*Continued*)

Table 2.1 (Continued)

Author(s) and year	*Principal research question*	*Methodology*	*Findings*
Muehling and Sprott (2004)	Do nostalgic cues in ads influence consumer thoughts and attitudes about the ad and the advertised brand?	Qualitative (projecting technique) and quantitative (survey research)	Exposure to nostalgic ad (as compared to an analogous non-nostalgic ad) positively influences attitudes about the ad and the advertised brand.
Reisenwitz, Iyer, and Cutler (2004)	What influence does nostalgia proneness have on nostalgia intensity towards print ads and brands?	Quantitative (survey research)	Consumers' nostalgia proneness is positively related to both nostalgia intensity towards the ad and the advertised brand.
Sierra and McQuitty (2007)	Can SIT explain the effects of nostalgia on purchase intensions (theoretical assumption)?	Quantitative (survey research)	Cognitive and emotional factors simultaneously determine consumers' intention to purchase nostalgia products.
Muehling, Sprott and Sultan (2014)	Does in-home exposure to the brand influences consumers' response to nostalgia-themed advertisement?	Qualitative (projecting technique) and quantitative (survey research)	Nostalgic advertisement is most likely to elicit a positive attitude towards such brand and hence increases the likelihood of purchase intention.
Grębosz-Krawczyk (2020)	What are the attitudes and behaviour of Polish consumers towards nostalgic brands, depending on the category of brands and the demographic characteristics of the consumers?	Qualitative (focus groups) and quantitative (survey research)	Transgenerational brands are perceived as ones of seemingly higher quality (as compared to generational brands). Moreover, the post-communist origin of the Polish respondents was not found to affect their attitudes and behaviour.

The approach for this study involved extensive searches of relevant business management and education online databases, namely SCOPUS, Web of Science, EBSCO, and ProQuest. These databases usually feature advanced search engines that allow one to enter complex search queries to narrow the scope of a search.[49] Hand searches and Internet searches were made as well to identify secondary references and further publications by authors reported in the search results. The intention was to ensure that all the literature in the field was found while keeping the focus on the literature of greatest relevance to the subject of the following dissertation to collect the 'best evidence' for the review.

The search was limited to the literature from 1990 to 2023. The starting date was chosen because it was in the 1990s when the world of science witnessed a new wave of scholarship devoted to the phenomenon of nostalgia in the context of marketing. However, had one considered the marvellous LEGO® story from 2004[50] to be the defining moment when nostalgia worked wonders in the toy industry, then the search would have been limited to just the past two decades of the 21st century. The review considered publications in the English language from the United Kingdom, the United States, France, the Netherlands, Austria, and Korea. Peer-reviewed journal papers based on empirical research were prioritised; unpublished management conference papers and other types of documents in professional publications were excluded.

The search resulted in 22 papers being selected for more detailed verification from 107 citations in total. However, most of the commonly cited works had mistakenly used the word 'toys' as referring to intercourse or sexual activities. Each publication was scrutinised for its significance to the guidelines of the applied methodology, and following strict application of the search parameters, only nine empirical research papers were selected for inclusion in this review. These studies exceed the scope of the present dissertation, though they share a common theme, that is, nostalgia and toys.

It is therefore evident that the investigation of nostalgia and its declared impact on the contemporaneous toy industry has not been studied thoroughly, thereby giving the author a chance to expand the scope of scholarship. A table summarising the aforementioned findings is provided in Table 2.2.

Of all the studies included in this systematic literature review, the one with the highest number of citations was the one by Morris and Martin.[51] The topic of this article centred around a line of stuffed toys being sold under the name of 'Beanie Babies'. Specifically, the authors found a relationship between a set of ten product attributes imbued into the plush toys, one of which was nostalgia and brand loyalty. Hence, a company such as Ty Inc. is said to foster a high-involvement relationship with its customers. The results of the survey research conducted on a group of 137 students indicated that BBs' toys were easily recognisable by the respondents and reminded them of fond childhood memories. Some individuals who admitted to collecting these palm-sized objects of play believed that one day they would bestow them to their children and grandchildren, which entails the presence of transgenerational cues. By sticking to their values, the manufacturer of BBs was found to effectively nurture consumer-product relationships by mustering the possibilities of nostalgia, which results in higher sales volumes.

In the next article, Kang et al.[52] focus on the emerging phenomenon of mature people who buy toys exclusively for themselves. The authors refer to these individuals as 'kidults' – a well-fitted wordplay describing a subject who has preserved a childlike heart inside a more grown body. Interestingly, such a kidult tends to buy objects of play without being noticed, thus taking pleasure in the shopping experience alone.

In another study involving Indian females, Wagner et al.[53] found that possession attachment towards global brands acquired during childhood does shape individuals' behaviourism and the way they see cultural roles. In this example, a Barbie doll has successfully introduced Western culture to Indian girls, thereby infringing on their customs and traditions that differ significantly from the transnational community of the modern world. The study included female subjects born between 1985 and 1998. Those participants who had a strong possession attachment resulting from nostalgia were more likely to develop preferences that led to the adoption of Western roles.

In the next article, '*Adult nostalgia and children's toys past and present*', Baxter[54] described the repetitive manner of releasing the same toys yet in an updated version. Specifically, she has reported that the perpetuation of certain toys is being made on purpose. Scarcely does a child represent the marketers' target audience since the industry has been attempting to allure the parents. In this way, a company strives to recapture these consumers who, as young children, hold pleasant memories surrounding a toy product or pursue their lost childhood. These tangible objects that are both a symbolic representation of childhood and one's lived past, at the same time, become tools in forming an intergenerational bond. In stark contrast, the fifth article offers a divergent view on recourse to maudlin sentimentality in marketing. Nabec[55] asserts that regardless of the approach, parents may develop three strategies to counter consumer socialisation of children. Participants alleged that every marketing endeavour not related to the product per se should be deemed deceptive. It is suggested that a toy that carries benefits for children does not need any psychological tricks in order to be purchased.

In his most recent paper by Sotelo-Duarte,[56] the author addressed the topic of nostalgic collecting behaviour in the context of interpersonal relations with other people. The study employed netnography, a digital version of ethnographic research, to provide a qualitative depiction of people collecting vintage toys. In the framework of the applied methodology, 40,000 online comments on YouTube were analysed from over 9,000 users. It was found that the collecting process consists of three stages: 'beginning of a collection', 'progression of a collection', and 'the end of the collecting process'.

Table 2.2 The results of systematic literature review on nostalgia in toy industry

Selection criteria	*Number of identified articles*			
	SCOPUS	*Web of Science*	*EBSCO*	*ProQuest*
'Nostalgia' AND 'toys' OR 'nostalgia' AND 'toy industry*' OR 'nostalgic' AND 'toys' OR 'nostalgic' AND 'toy industry*' – title	0	1	1	0
'Nostalgia' AND 'toys' OR 'nostalgia' AND 'toy industry*' OR 'nostalgic' AND 'toys' OR 'nostalgic' AND 'toy industry' – abstract	1	8	10	4
'Nostalgia' AND 'toys' OR 'nostalgia' AND 'toy industry*' OR 'nostalgic' AND 'toys' OR 'nostalgic' AND 'toy industry*' – keywords	0	4	3	0
In total: elimination of duplicates	22			
Verification of abstracts in terms of the leading subject of research – nostalgia and toy industry	9			

Moreover, it emerged that collectors are aroused to behave in such a way because of the social impact of people in their circle. Such findings seem to be in line with those of Sierra and McQuitty,[57] whereby being part of an ephemeral collective entity at some point in the past affects the purchase of nostalgic products (in the context of this study, toys).

The last three articles by Moran,[58] Cross,[59] and LaRocca[60] are merely essays and present authors' personal opinions on the issues such as remediation of children's culture, the new role of collectible toys and dolls as symbolic embodiments of an idealised childhood, and a new trend in modern architecture whereby buildings resemble kids' brick construction as made with LEGO®.[61]

2.4 Chapter summary

Given the competitive setting of the modern market, a company must retain its perceived superiority over other firms engaged in a fierce rivalry. Positioning a nostalgic brand through references to the collective history and premeditated fabrication of the past to hold the attention of customers builds a sense of credibility and trust (authenticity), thereby placing a company in a strategically advantageous position as compared to non-nostalgic options in the current market. Positioning is, in essence, the process of determining the place of a brand's products in the market, solidifying its brand image in the minds of target buyers, and communicating its identity to consumers. In addition, the concept of positioning involves emphasising a brand's unique instrumental utilities and values that differentiate it from competitors and impel consumers to choose it. Nostalgic brand positioning, in particular, is predicated on the brand's historical background and target audience, whereby positive emotions are aroused by invoking familiar events from the past on the basis of the continuities that constitute their significance at present. The goal is to create a clear, precise, and unique nostalgic image in the mind of the target consumer.

In all, this leads to the conclusion that nostalgia is a crucial element of the contemporary positioning strategy oriented on the utilisation of the subjectively created past as an asset enhancing a selling proposition. Linking the brand with the customers' shared past may increase the brand's nostalgic value by developing a distinctive brand image, which effectively differentiates the brand from the competitors and thus increases customers' interaction with the merchandise.

In the literature, there has been little discussion about the impact of nostalgia on brand management in the toy industry, nonetheless.

Notes

1 Heinberg et al., "How Nostalgic Brand Positioning Shapes Brand Equity: Differences between Emerging and Developed Markets", 870.
2 Holbrook and Schindler, "Age, Sex, and Attitude Toward the Past as Predictors of Consumers' Aesthetic Tastes for Cultural Products", 412–422.
3 Aaker, *Building Strong Brands*, 70.
4 Grębosz-Krawczyk, "The Impact of Nostalgia on Brand Equity in a Post-Communist Economy", 218–222.
5 Grębosz-Krawczyk, *Nostalgia w Zarządzaniu Marką*, 191–192.
6 Kessous and Roux, "A Semiotic Analysis of Nostalgia as a Connection to the Past", 192–212; Brown, "Retro Galore! Is There No End to Nostalgia?", 9–29; Breen and Robertson, *Brick by Brick: How LEGO Rewrote the Rules of Innovation and Conquered the Global Toy Industry.*
7 Merchant and Rose, "Effects of Advertising-Evoked Vicarious Nostalgia on Brand Heritage", 2621.
8 Brown et al., "Teaching Old Brands New Tricks: Retro Branding and the Revival of Brand Meaning", 20.
9 Holbrook, "Nostalgia and Consumption Preferences: Some Emerging Patterns of Consumer Tastes", 245.
10 Grębosz-Krawczyk, *Nostalgia w Zarządzaniu Marką*, 183.
11 Grębosz-Krawczyk, *Nostalgia w Zarządzaniu Marką*, 186.
12 Braun et al., "Make My Memory: How Advertising Can Change Our Memories of the Past", 1–23.
13 Brown, "Retro Galore! Is There No End to Nostalgia?", 12.
14 Routledge, *Nostalgia: A Psychological Resource*, 6.
15 Holbrook and Schindler, "Some Exploratory Findings on the Development of Musical Tastes", 119–124.
16 Holbrook, "Nostalgia and Consumption Preferences: Some Emerging Patterns of Consumer Tastes", 245.

17 Holbrook and Schindler, "Some Exploratory Findings on the Development of Musical Tastes", 122.
18 Holbrook, "Nostalgia and Consumption Preferences: Some Emerging Patterns of Consumer Tastes", 247.
19 Holbrook and Schindler, "Age, Sex, and Attitude Toward the Past as Predictors of Consumers' Aesthetic Tastes for Cultural Products", 412.
20 Routledge, *Nostalgia: A Psychological Resource*, 40.
21 Havlena and Holak, "'The Good Old Days': Observations on Nostalgia and Its Role in Consumer Behavior", 323.
22 Stern, "Historical and Personal Nostalgia in Advertising Text: The Fin de Siècle Effect", 11.
23 Holbrook and Schindler, "Age, Sex, and Attitude Toward the Past as Predictors of Consumers' Aesthetic Tastes for Cultural Products", 412.
24 Holak and Havlena, "Nostalgia: An Exploratory Study of Themes and Emotions in the Nostalgic Experience", 380.
25 Havlena and Holak, "'The Good Old Days': Observations on Nostalgia and Its Role in Consumer Behavior", 326.
26 Holak and Havlena, "Feelings, Fantasies, and Memories: An Examination of the Emotional Components of Nostalgia", 217.
27 Routledge, *Nostalgia: A Psychological Resource*, 15–16.
28 Routledge, *Nostalgia: A Psychological Resource*, 16.
29 Pascal et al., "The Influence of Evoked Nostalgia on Consumers' Responses to Advertising: An Exploratory Study", 39.
30 Reisenwitz et al., "Nostalgia Advertising and the Influence of Nostalgia Proneness", 55.
31 Reisenwitz et al., "Nostalgia Advertising and the Influence of Nostalgia Proneness", 58.
32 Holbrook and Schindler, "Age, Sex, and Attitude Toward the Past as Predictors of Consumers' Aesthetic Tastes for Cultural Products", 414–415.
33 Pascal et al., "The Influence of Evoked Nostalgia on Consumers' Responses to Advertising: An Exploratory Study", 42–43.
34 Baker and Kennedy, "Death by Nostalgia: A Diagnosis of Context-Specific Cases", 169–174.
35 Sierra and McQuitty, "Attitudes and Emotions as Determinants of Nostalgia Purchases: An Application of Social Identity Theory", 100.
36 Sierra and McQuitty, "Attitudes and Emotions as Determinants of Nostalgia Purchases: An Application of Social Identity Theory", 100–112.
37 Muehling et al., "Exploring the Boundaries of Nostalgic Advertising Effects: A Consideration of Childhood Brand Exposure and Attachment on Consumers' Responses to Nostalgia-Themed Advertisements", 73.
38 Pascal et al., "The Influence of Evoked Nostalgia on Consumers' Responses to Advertising: An Exploratory Study", 39–47.
39 Grębosz-Krawczyk, *Nostalgia w Zarządzaniu Marką*.
40 Grębosz-Krawczyk, *Nostalgia w Zarządzaniu Marką*.
41 Aaker, *Building Strong Brands*, 8.
42 Kessous et al., "Consumer–Brand Relationships: A Contrast of Nostalgic and Non-Nostalgic Brands", 187–202.
43 Batcho, "Nostalgia: A Psychological Perspective", 131–143.

44 Kessous et al., "Consumer–Brand Relationships: A Contrast of Nostalgic and Non-Nostalgic Brands", 187.
45 Brown et al., "Teaching Old Brands New Tricks: Retro Branding and the Revival of Brand Meaning", 19.
46 Unger et al., "The Use of Nostalgia in Television Advertising: A Content Analysis", 347.
47 Routledge, *Nostalgia: A Psychological Resource*, 39.
48 Czakon et al., "Krótkowzroczność Strategiczna – Metodyczne Aspekty Systematycznego Przeglądu Literatury", 30.
49 Czakon et al., "Krótkowzroczność Strategiczna – Metodyczne Aspekty Systematycznego Przeglądu Literatury", 34.
50 Lubiński, "The Study of Nostalgia-Oriented Strategy Aimed at Millennials on the Example of the LEGO Group", 90.
51 Morris and Martin, "Beanie Babies: A Case Study in the Engineering of a High-Involvement/Relationship-Prone Brand", 78–98.
52 Kang et al., "Motivation and Behavior of Kidult Consumers' Toy Consumption", 41.
53 Wagner et al., "Possession Attachment Toward Global Brands: How the 'World of Barbie' Is Shaping the Mindsets of Millennial Girls", 440.
54 Baxter, "Adult Nostalgia and Children's Toys Past and Present", 230–231.
55 Nabec, "Les formes de résistance parentale à la consommation enfantine et au kids marketing", 163–164.
56 Sotelo-Duarte, "Collecting Nostalgic Pieces of Plastic: The Journey of Toy Collectors and the Effects of Nostalgia", 319–336.
57 Sierra and McQuitty, "Attitudes and Emotions as Determinants of Nostalgia Purchases: An Application of Social Identity Theory", 109.
58 Moran, "Childhood and Nostalgia in Contemporary Culture", 155–175.
59 Cross, "Nostalgic Collections", 101–106.
60 LaRocca, "Legocentism", 76–89.
61 LaRocca, "Legocentism", 80–81.

Reference list

Aaker, David A. *Building Strong Brands*. New York: Free Press, 1996.

Baker, Stacey Menzel., and Patrizia Kennedy. "Death by Nostalgia: A Diagnosis of Context-Specific Cases." *Advances in Consumer Research* 21 (1994): 169–174.

Batcho, Krystine I. "Nostalgia: A Psychological Perspective." *Perceptual and Motor Skills* 80, no. 1 (1995): 131–143. https://doi.org/10.2466/pms.1995.80.1.131.

Baxter, Jane E. "Adult Nostalgia and Children's Toys Past and Present." *International Journal of Play* 5, no. 3 (2016): 230–243. https://doi.org/10.1080/21594937.2016.1220046.

Braun, Kathryn A., Rhiannon Ellis, and Elizabeth F. Loftus. "Make My Memory: How Advertising Can Change Our Memories of the Past." *Psychology & Marketing* 19, no. 1 (2002): 1–23. https://doi.org/10.1002/mar.1000.

Breen, Bill, and David Robertson. *Brick by Brick: How LEGO Rewrote the Rules of Innovation and Conquered the Global Toy Industry*. New York: Random House Business Books, 2013.

Brown, Stephen. "Retro Galore! Is There No End to Nostalgia?" *Journal of Customer Behaviour* 17, no. 1–2 (2018): 9–29. https://doi.org/10.1362/147539218X15208755279216.

Brown, Stephen, Robert Kozinets, and John Sherry. "Teaching Old Brands New Tricks: Retro Branding and the Revival of Brand Meaning." *Journal of Marketing* 67 (2003): 19–33.

Cross, Gary. "Nostalgic Collections." *Consumption Markets & Culture* 20, no. 2 (2017): 101–106. https://doi.org/10.1080/10253866.2016.1167469.

Czakon, Wojciech, Patrycja Klimas, and Arkadiusz Kawa. "Krótkowzroczność Strategiczna – Metodyczne Aspekty Systematycznego Przeglądu Literatury." *Studia Oeconomica Posnaniensia* 7, no. 2 (2019): 27–37. https://doi.org/10.18559/SOEP.2019.2.2.

Grębosz-Krawczyk, Magdalena. "The Impact of Nostalgia on Brand Equity in a Post-Communist Economy." *Economics and Sociology* 11, no. 2 (2018): 216–228. https://doi.org/10.14254/2071-789X.2018/11-2/15.

Grębosz-Krawczyk, Magdalena. *Nostalgia w Zarządzaniu Marką*. Warsaw: Wydawnictwo C.H. Beck, 2020.

Havlena, William J., and Susan L. Holak. "The Good Old Days: Observations on Nostalgia and Its Role in Consumer Behavior." *Advances in Consumer Research* 18 (1991): 323–329.

Heinberg, Martin, Constantine S. Katsikeas, H. Erkan Ozkaya, and Markus Taube. "How Nostalgic Brand Positioning Shapes Brand Equity: Differences Between Emerging and Developed Markets." *Journal of the Academy of Marketing Science* 48, no. 5 (2020): 869–890. https://doi.org/10.1007/s11747-019-00637-x.

Holak, Susan L., and William J. Havlena. "Nostalgia: An Exploratory Study of Themes and Emotions in the Nostalgic Experience." *Advances in Consumer Research* 19, no. 1 (1992): 380–387.

Holak, Susan L., and William J. Havlena. "Feelings, Fantasies, and Memories: An Examination of the Emotional Components of Nostalgia." *Journal of Business Research* 42, no. 3 (1998): 217–226. https://doi.org/10.1016/S0148-2963(97)00119-7.

Holbrook, Morris B. "Nostalgia and Consumption Preferences: Some Emerging Patterns of Consumer Tastes." *Journal of Consumer Research* 20, no. 2 (1993): 245–256. https://doi.org/10.1086/209346.

Holbrook, Morris B., and Robert M. Schindler. "Some Exploratory Findings on the Development of Musical Tastes." *Journal of Consumer Research* 16, no. 1 (1989): 119–124. https://doi.org/10.1086/209200.

Holbrook, Morris B., and Robert M. Schindler. "Age, Sex, and Attitude Toward the Past as Predictors of Consumers' Aesthetic Tastes for Cultural Products." *Journal of Marketing Research* 31, no. 3 (1994): 412–422. https://doi.org/10.2307/3152227.

Kang, Seunghee, Jesung Lee, and June Lee. "Motivation and Behavior of Kidult Consumers' Toy Consumption." *Journal of Consumption Culture* 23, no. 1 (2020): 41–65. https://doi.org/10.17053/jcc.2020.23.1.003

Kessous, Aurélie, and Elyette Roux. "A Semiotic Analysis of Nostalgia as a Connection to the Past." *Qualitative Market Research: An International Journal* 11, no. 2 (2008): 192–212.

Kessous, Aurélie, Elyette Roux, and Jean-Louis Chandon. "Consumer–Brand Relationships: A Contrast of Nostalgic and Non-Nostalgic Brands." *Psychology & Marketing* 32, no. 2 (2015): 187–202. https://doi.org/10.1002/mar.20772.

LaRocca, David. "Legocentrism." *The Senses and Society* 12, no. 1 (2017): 76–89. https://doi.org/10.1080/17458927.2017.1268824.

Lubiński, Kamil. "The Study of Nostalgia-Oriented Strategy Aimed at Millennials on the Example of the LEGO Group." *Journal of Intercultural Management* 12, no. 2 (2020): 86–105. https://doi.org/10.2478/joim-2020-0039.

Merchant, Altaf, and Gregory M. Rose. "Effects of Advertising-Evoked Vicarious Nostalgia on Brand Heritage." *Journal of Business Research* 66, no. 12 (2013): 2619–2625. https://doi.org/10.1016/j.jbusres.2012.05.021.

Moran, Joe. "Childhood and Nostalgia in Contemporary Culture." *European Journal of Cultural Studies* 5, no. 2 (2002): 155–173. https://doi.org/10.1177/1364942002005002338.

Morris, Rebecca J., and Charles L. Martin. "Beanie Babies: A Case Study in the Engineering of a High-Involvement/Relationship-Prone Brand." *Journal of Product & Brand Management* 9, no. 2 (2000): 78–98. https://doi.org/10.1108/10610420010322143.

Muehling, Darrel D., David E. Sprott, and Abdullah J. Sultan. "Exploring the Boundaries of Nostalgic Advertising Effects: A Consideration of Childhood Brand Exposure and Attachment on Consumers' Responses to Nostalgia-Themed Advertisements." *Journal of Advertising* 43, no. 1 (2014): 73–84. https://doi.org/10.1080/00913367.2013.815110.

Nabec, Lydiane. "Les formes de résistance parentale à la consommation enfantine et au kids marketing." *Management & Avenir* 60, no. 2 (2013): 157–175. https://doi.org/10.3917/mav.060.0157.

Pascal, Vincent, David E. Sprott, and Darrel D. Muehling. "The Influence of Evoked Nostalgia on Consumers' Responses to Advertising: An Exploratory Study." *Journal of Current Issues and Research in Advertising* 24, no. 1 (2002): 39–47.

Reisenwitz, Timothy H., Rajesh Iyer, and Bob Cutler. "Nostalgia Advertising and the Influence of Nostalgia Proneness." *Marketing Management Journal* 14, no. 2 (2004): 55–66.

Routledge, Clay. *Nostalgia: A Psychological Resource.* New York: Routledge, 2016.

Sierra, Jeremy J., and Shaun McQuitty. "Attitudes and Emotions as Determinants of Nostalgia Purchases: An Application of Social Identity Theory." *Journal of Marketing Theory and Practice* 15, no. 2 (2007): 99–112. https://doi.org/10.2753/MTP1069-6679150201.

Sotelo-Duarte, Manuel. "Collecting Nostalgic Pieces of Plastic: The Journey of Toy Collectors and the Effects of Nostalgia." *Qualitative Market Research* 25, no. 2 (2022): 319–336. https://doi.org/10.1108/QMR-07-2021-0090.

Stern, Barbara B. "Historical and Personal Nostalgia in Advertising Text: The Fin de Siècle Effect." *Journal of Advertising* 21, no. 4 (1992): 11–22.

Unger, Lynette S., Diane M. Mcconocha, and John A. Faier. "The Use of Nostalgia in Television Advertising: A Content Analysis." *Journalism Quarterly* 68, no. 3 (1991): 345–353.

Wagner, Udo, Isaac Jacob, Monica Khanna, and Krupa A. Rai. "Possession Attachment Toward Global Brands: How the 'World of Barbie' Is Shaping the Mindsets of Millennial Girls." *Journal of International Consumer Marketing* 33, no. 4 (2021): 434–451. https://doi.org/10.1080/08961530.2020.1813671.

3 Consumers' motivations and behaviours in the context of nostalgia-oriented purchase

3.1 Consumer perception of nostalgic brands

Consumers differ in how they perceive brands, as each individual holds a subjective view of reality. This perception process is critical for understanding and influencing consumer behaviour. Central to the process of brand perception are so-called schemas – networks of associations linked to a brand, product, store, or other objects.[1] In a schema, a brand is associated with a range of positive or negative qualities and sensations. The sources of schemas include one's own experiences, other people's experiences, and information from personal, commercial, and public sources.

In psychology, perception is defined as a complex cognitive process that results in the formation of an image of reality in the human mind. Perception is not a passive representation of reality but an active and creative process. Its essence lies in organising the material provided by the senses into a coherent whole. Internal patterns of reality, formed on the basis of previous experience, play a fundamental role in perception.

Harrell[2] defines perception as the process of recognising, selecting, organising, and interpreting stimuli. Since perception involves identifying rather than passively registering information – and often goes beyond the data provided – it is possible to accurately recognise brands even when there are gaps in sensory input. Our differing perceptions of brands stem from variations in attitudes and behaviours.

The five senses play a crucial role in the perception process. Beyond the mere perception of sensory impressions, an equally important aspect of perception is interpretation. This involves an individual's attribution of socio-psychological meanings to a perceived object, such as a brand.[3] In the process of perception, a network of associations facilitates the processing of information through reception, storage in memory, recognition, and recall. Consumers differ in how they perceive brands, with perceptions influenced by factors such as prior knowledge, the consumer's orientation (related to their search for a specific product category), the context of their situation, cognitive style, expectations, and level of involvement. Individual differences

DOI: 10.4324/9781003606079-5

also stem from subjective experiences, personal life histories, and current circumstances.[4]

Referring to perceptual theory, it can be said that the way brands are perceived in terms of the nostalgia they evoke depends on the consumer's personal experiences from childhood, youth, or adulthood, as well as historically significant events specific to a particular generation. Most nostalgic brands aim to evoke positive emotions, which, in turn, facilitate straightforward decision-making.

The study of emotional processes is particularly relevant to consumer behaviour towards nostalgic brands, as emotions mediate or play a role in various processes related to brand recognition and choice. Moreover, emotions can influence and shape specific attitudes towards brands. A consumer's attitude towards a brand can be defined as an overall evaluation of the brand, encompassing feelings about specific brand attributes such as quality, functionality, image, attractiveness, price, availability, reliability, and innovation.[5] Attitudes are either learnt or acquired and are formed as a result of one's own experiences or the shared experiences communicated by others.[6] Consequently, a consumer's past and the experiences of those close to them can shape attitudes towards brands associated with the 'good old days'. However, attitudes, as a person's tendency to form judgements, can be shaped and changed over time.

Most consumer attitudes are formed according to the standard hierarchy of cognition, which implies significant consumer involvement in the purchase process. Consumers approach the decision to purchase a particular product as a problem-solving process. They first form beliefs about the product by gathering information about its attributes, then evaluate these beliefs, feelings, and emotions, and finally take specific actions regarding the product. This approach to product selection often leads to brand loyalty. In contrast, under the low-involvement hierarchy, consumers rarely develop a strong preference for a particular brand. Brand choice is generally passive, driven by incentives such as promotional pricing, attractive packaging, product placement, or the convenience of spending minimal time and effort on the decision. Only after purchasing and trying the product do consumers form opinions about it and develop attitudes. Attitudes influenced by a hedonistic approach to consumption are primarily based on emotions. After the purchase, customers begin to recognise additional benefits of the product. Feelings and emotions associated with the brand, combined with the user's personal experiences, serve as the foundation for the formation of attitudes towards the brand. These attitudes are often rooted in intangible attributes.[7]

The formation of a brand attitude occurs at the moment of first contact, making the brand message and brand identifiers crucial. However, at later stages, a change in attitude may occur, influenced by acquired knowledge about the brand, personal experiences, the opinions of others, or the context of purchase or use.

Kessous et Roux,[8] based on their analysis of interviews with potential consumers, identified four types of nostalgic behaviour among consumers:

- Kidult: adults belonging to Generation X or Y, who yearn for childhood. Born during the rapid spread of new technologies but still rooted in traditional values, this group associates nostalgia with security. Consuming brands from their past helps them feel comforted, particularly as they recall global crises and the duality of progress.
- Traditionalist: members of the Breakthrough Generation (1968–1978), born during European social transformation. This group matured later, gained higher education, and started families and careers later than previous generations. For them, nostalgia fulfils a need for reference points, often tied to authentic brands associated with significant life events. For this group, value authenticity over imitation, as 'fakes' lack the power to evoke genuine memories.
- Proponent of Change: this group primarily includes representatives of the Baby Boomer generation (1948–1967), who strongly support the principles of capitalism, entrepreneurship, private property, and freedom. For them, nostalgia plays a key role in defining and maintaining their identity, primarily fulfilling their need for independence.
- Intergenerational: this group is mainly represented by the interwar generation (1928–1947). For people nearing the end of their lives, nostalgia satisfies the need to reflect and remember. It is often triggered by personal objects from their past.

Regardless of the sociological concepts or constructs that would further explain particular consumer behaviour, it is still useless intelligence unless the main reason is unveiled – a key to understanding the simplest and yet the most indescribable content of 'why'.[9] Why do people behave in such a way? Why do they choose to belong to certain cognitive entities? Why do they decide to buy nostalgic products? Why do men and women do what they do? Or simpler, what *drives* them to do so? Motivation is arguably the most salient concept in psychology and research on consumer behaviour.

3.2 Consumer motivation theories and nostalgia concept

Motivation can be defined as 'the set of factors stimulating consumers to initiate, direct, and maintain a particular activity'.[10] Because of the entanglement of internal and external factors, motivation is therefore said to be a complex process.

Some of the old theories presumed that an individual's behaviour is directed through external motivation. More recent theories emphasise the crucial role of aesthetic cues, such as the external impression, in shaping consumer preferences.[11] On a primary level, instincts and impulses are, according to many in the field of behavioural research, conceded to be the fundamentals of motivation. However, when speaking of the more humanistic approach, motivation is determined by needs and wants.

When Davis introduced his concept of nostalgia, many scholars demanded proof that such behaviour is not merely a matter of happy accident. Although his findings were convincing enough to the marketing practitioners, researchers were somewhat sceptical that day.[12] Had he already revealed the solution, which was clearly on his doorstep, the research on nostalgia would probably not have seen its massive resurgence in the 1990s. 'Motivation' is a term that conveys all the answers to these unanswered questions regarding not only nostalgia but also essentially consumer behaviour in its entirety.

Motivation is an internal process and refers to contemporaneous factors that ignite and cause an individual's actions.[13] Comparable with Social Identity Theory, previous experiences also play a fundamental role when speaking of an individual's disposition to behave in a certain way. However, contrary to the idea of learning (a result of training and practice), motivation is ahistorical in orientation, thereby meaning that the final outcome is what concerns most and how it influences locomotion, energy, and persistence.[14] In other words, motivation is a process of attaining a goal.[15] Atkinson[16] writes that the concept of motivation is surrounded by three coexistent themes: want, desire, and wish. Want emphasises the state of lacking something. Desire refers to the fervour of feelings. Wish expresses the unattainable object in the present. No matter what this object of interest might be, an individual may feel either attraction or aversion towards the pursuit. Accordingly, people are attracted to experiences that enhance their self-concept (e.g., provide them with a source of satisfaction) and shall refrain from those that might be unsatisfactory. Thus, the subject's response to behave in a certain way emanates from inner impulses that stimulate a particular action. Despite being treated independently as a singular construct, motivation by no means should be conjectured thus and so, given that people are galvanised into action by different drivers.[17]

From the above, it appears that motivation works on the principle of the action-reaction cycle. Action is usually followed by an intention aimed at attaining some conscious end, an objective. Once obtained, the measure of an individual's want is filled up, rewarded. James[18] had written much earlier that the presence of an already defined desire influences locomotion towards gratification. It follows, therefore, that wants and desires are a source of exquisite pleasure, and exactly it is this pleasantness that serves as a force for an individual to sway his behaviour, thus yielding pleasure within an individual. Perhaps this is why Hirschman and Holbrook (as cited in Childers et al., 2001)[19] regarded consumers as individual souls 'seeking fun, fantasy, arousal, sensory stimulation and enjoyment'. Following in the same vein, Westbrook and Black[20] have found that consumption, shopping, takes place not only for the sake of acquiring goods but also for satisfying one's needs.

At this point, it would be deeply inappropriate not to include Maslow's renowned hierarchy of needs – a theory that for good has been inherited in the canon of social sciences literature. Back in the 1940s, Abraham Maslow,[21] interested in how people attain the so-called peak experiences, proposed an idea whereby on no account is it possible for a subject to satisfy his need unless an earlier one has been completed. Thus, Maslow has conveyed it by forming a pyramid encompassing biogenic and psychogenic needs. There are five different levels of Maslow's hierarchy of needs, and these can be further classified into deficiency and growth needs. Ideally, it is said that individuals advance gradually through each level, moving from the bottom and ascending the peak. The ultimate goal, therefore, is to reach the fifth level of the pyramid: self-actualisation. However, much later, Maslow[22] admitted this statement to be inaccurate and misleading, given a strong criticism from the psychologists claiming that his theory would work only in typical western societies such as the United States.[23] Solomon et al.,[24] in particular, have noted that Maslow's hierarchy is culture-bound, meaning that the order of the pyramid, which was supposed to be fixed, is disrupted among other cultures. Naturally, it was not long until marketers went farther than Maslow for the sake of understanding consumer motivation. Specifically, they delved into the idea of amalgamation whereby a product would satisfy all the needs from the pyramid.[25] Although this somewhat simplistic methodology, overwhelmed by a hunger for profits, distorted the originator's thought, unconsciously, it managed to maintain the notion by which one's priorities are dynamic.[26] Today Maslow's hierarchy of needs attracts a steady stream of business students seeking the explanation of human motivation.

Maslow seems to have preceded his times, for although the vast majority of researchers view the pyramid of needs as a quaint relic stripped of much contemporary significance, he has adjusted to the modern evolutionary trends of human motivation and cognition. That is, how can one be motivated to locomote in recurrent adaptive situations?[27] In such a case, the theory is consistent with functional analyses. Nevertheless, it cannot be denied that regardless of the uncritical acceptance of Maslow's hierarchy of needs theory, the result of which was no single study over a span of nearly 30 years,[28] it has become one of the most cognitively contagious ideas, implying the importance of discerning one's wants and needs. It was not until then that marketers embraced this perspective to use it to their advantage because it indirectly indicates the types of products whose benefits are in demand given various stages of customers' motivation and resources. Following recent trends in developmental psychology, it means that there are different domain-specific motivational systems for each motive in the hierarchy. Successful marketing is therefore oriented on identifying the wants and needs not only of core customers but also of the potential audience a company may reach.

It has been customary for marketers to believe that the lookout for new insights would help them better understand patterns of consumer behaviour economically, politically, sociologically, and humanly.[29] This has, in turn, given rise to a new trend of 'psychographic segmentation typologies' where individuals are being categorised by age, income, level of education, and other quantitative variables. Now that such analyses have allowed marketers to look inside customers' profiles, companies may use these data to steer customers towards particular products or adjust their endeavours to respond to their current needs. Thus, following Shih,[30] since people display different lifestyles and media usage, proper selection of media units combined with the accurate tuning to peak viewing time significantly contributes to the success of advertising techniques. To gather such data, companies and research agencies develop their own segmentation typologies. These usually encompass customers' shaped perceptions on subjects, including brands, celebrities, and preferences. Once collected, the data are then being sold to potential companies willing to learn more about their clients. Generally, these typologies are of the same nature, sharing the common feature of dividing the population into five to ten segments.[31] Each 'profile' then receives a descriptive name and concise definition. Rarely are researchers able to compare such typologies, mainly due to the confidential character of the data. Disclosing such sensitive information would adversely affect the company. One of the commonly used market segmentation tools is the 'assessment of values', given the belief of consumer researchers that the relationship exists between values and the purchase of specific products.[32]

Why have values gained so much attention recently? In short, because they affect every aspect of living. Values, following the view proposed by Shrum et al.,[33] 'serve to guide actions, attitudes and judgments and therefore are determinants of attitudes as well as behaviour'. They are perpetual beliefs whereby an individual chooses to locomote in a certain way as the preferable option to an opposing mode of conduct. Values, therefore, place the environment in which behaviour occurs (i.e., represented in the life space) on the approval-disapproval continuum.[34] Moreover, elements such as affection, cognition, and conation are fundamental to the concept of value. People refer to values when an individual approaches a situation of which the consequences are unknown in the long run or when one has to choose between what he 'would do' and what he 'ought to do', keeping in mind the social constraints. In other words, then, every change of behaviour manifested as the movement of activity should be regarded as a compromise between motivation and the psychological environment (as conceived by Lewin)[35] in value terms. When living in a society, it is adamant that interaction between the subject and his environment satisfies the norms. Otherwise, such a person shall not receive expectable feedback, meaning that he would not be able to get what he wants from other group members in personal and emotional terms.[36]

Similarly to culture, values are based on what has been said and done by subjects but 'represent' a cognitive and affective dimension of the sense data. They offer an element of predictability to the social sphere, as stressed by Kluckhohn.[37] In the same spirit, Beatty et al.[38] wrote that values provide information on how a society operates, mainly due to a perception that they play a pivotal role in people's psychological makeup. It has been argued that if a researcher wanted to gain a sociological view on customers' culture, investigating their values would be a convenient starting point.[39] This demonstrates why values have been dominating market research since the 1970s. VALS and its latest successor, VALS 2, are examples of a marketing methodology developed to segment people based on their lifestyles and values. They are believed to portray homogeneous patterns of consumer behaviour.[40] It is as if corporations got a representative image of 'who' the core customers are and 'what' their habits are. More recently, values have been found to influence television viewing habits, customer decision criteria, brand choice, store choice, and many more.[41]

Like any abstract psychological conceptualisations, values alone are difficult to measure even with the available systems of mathematics. However, when taking a different approach, in which a value focuses on a specific object that would accrue benefits in consumer terms, it forms an attitude.[42] Further, such attitudes implicitly reveal patterns of motivation that could not be so obvious when considering the income-related aspects of consumer behaviour singly. Solomon[43] writes that people use products to define lifestyles, which fits well with Veblen's[44] theory about 'conspicuous consumption'. A linkage of psychological attitudes with key demographics has been empirically verified to be employed in commercial applications.[45] Therefore, it is evident that marketers must identify assortments of products that consumers associate with a 'predictable' pattern of behaviour.

VALS was developed with the assumption that individuals with shared psychological profiles acquire a predictable set of products to encode and communicate their social role. It breaks up the population into eight segments based on their distinctive consumption patterns.[46] The framework, of which shape resembles a hexagonal structure, groups the subjects perpendicularly by 'resources' and horizontally by 'primary motivation'. A profile of a specific customer type is established based on a cross-sectional analysis of primary motivations and available resources. For example, depending on the degree of their inner resources, individuals that are motivated primarily by 'ideals' (driven by knowledge and principles) may be identified as either *Thinkers* or *Believers*. A notable exception includes two opposite edges of the hexagon. *Innovators*, who are at the top of the model, have a sufficient amount of resources such that they can be motivated by each of the three aforementioned primary motivations. On the contrary, *Survivors* display a high degree of complacency, thus significantly lacking any motivation or desire.[47] Although it has been demonstrated twice[48] on the example of five European countries that

American VALS could be utilised for international markets, SRI International has developed autonomous frameworks for six countries considering culture and cultural diversities. VALS gathers the data from their own-developed survey questionnaire composed of 34 questions.[49]

Within the VALS 2[50] model, three types of motivation have been identified: *principle-oriented motivation* (which is manifested in the pursuit of reliable merchandise and brands that have proven themselves in the past), *status-oriented motivation* (whereby an individual demonstrates a desire to own brands that resonate with his self-image), and *action-oriented motivation* (expressed in searching for new experiences).

The Customer Satisfaction Strategy model, on the other hand, presumes that consumers vary depending on their dominant needs. Callebaut et al.[51] theorise that the needs for play, control, affiliation, and status should be considered 'basic needs', while the need to stand out, the need for vitality, the need for inner peace, and the need to share are deemed 'complementary needs'. Nonetheless, the way the subject is going to satisfy these needs may differ in many aspects, beginning with one's personality traits and disposition and ending with common environmental impacts.

3.3 Types of consumers' motivation in the light of the concept of Nostalgia

In his conceptualisation of motivation, Solomon et al.[52] proposed that need may be utilitarian or hedonic. The former refers to the most generic goal of the consumption process, which is completing a purchase. The latter represents enjoyment and fun arising from the shopping experience, simply emotional worth.[53] As he further notes, these two types of need feature a paradoxical state of a discrepancy between the present state and some ideal state at some point in the future. This state provokes an inner conflict, one that stimulates the urge to stop it at once and return to the state of homeostasis.[54] The strength of the incitement, the extent to which a person is willing to devote energy to satisfy the longing, is called a *drive*.

Intrinsic and extrinsic motivation

Ryan and Deci's[55] Self-Determination Theory (SDT) sees a distinction between intrinsic and extrinsic motivation. The first type is said to be the closest to human nature, given the degree of autonomy one has in displaying a particular behaviour. It happens because when an individual grows and develops, it is curiosity that pushes him to gain knowledge and skills, or as Ryan[56] has described it, 'an inherent tendency to seek out novelty and changes'. Some researchers have been claiming that intrinsic motivation confines itself within the days of childhood, which is remarkably unspoiled at that period; however, the truth is more confusing, for an already developed pattern of behaviour models future locomotion in case an individual indulges an evocative passion that would conduce to satisfaction of the need for competence from doing such an activity.[57] It follows, therefore, that when an individual feels competent in what he is doing, he is catalysed to intrinsic motivation. Intrinsic motivation does not need any external incentives or rewards whatsoever. Contrary to the operant theory whereby an individual's behaviour is encouraged by external rewards, activities employed under intrinsic motivation are indeed a reward in themselves. Furthermore, unlike the previously mentioned concept of learning, intrinsic motivation does not need psychological drives.

Despite being the most salient and authentic type of motivation, intrinsic motivation becomes undermined when people are required to perform tasks that do not necessarily swell their enthusiasm. Usually, things begin to change after childhood as an individual's autonomy is fragile to the pressure of social demands.[58] That is why extrinsic motivation focuses on instrumental value, a separable outcome, rather than enjoyment of the experience itself.[59] Following the Self-Determination Theory (SDT) concept, extrinsic motivation ought to foster both internalisation and integration so that an individual turns his unwillingness towards a specific activity into personal engagement to do it either way. In other words, the process of internalisation is a desirable outcome of making a subject close to a state of inherent motivation.[60] It follows, therefore, that the greater the internalisation, the better the quality of one's engagement. Regardless, SDT is just a fraction of a much fuller theory of OIT (Organismic Integration Theory), whereby extrinsic motivation is divided into parts that vary in the degree to which an individual is motivated.[61] According to earlier conceptualisations that have treated motivation unitarily, motivation used to be categorised simply into 'amotivation' and 'motivation'. However, once an individual takes a detailed look into the elements of the OIT concept, he shall see that the space between the state of being unmotivated and motivated is immensely high.

External regulation is a heteronomous form of motivation. Because some activities do not rouse an individual's interest in doing it, as he would when intrinsically motivated, a stimulus is needed such that a person recognises the locomotion as a contingency between the progression and an external reward.[62] As a result, people are 'regulated' to behave in a certain way with the concerns of either obtaining this tangible reward or avoiding an undesired penalty.

Other levels of extrinsic motivation rely on the already mentioned idea of internalisation so that any forms of instrumentalities would no longer be of use. Despite apparent dichotomies within the concept questioning whether or not a regulation has been truly internalised, SDT predicts controlled-autonomous categorisation (levels) to illustrate gradual advancement towards behaviour that seems almost intrinsically motivated.[63] Ryan and Deci[64] labelled these processes as 'introjection', 'identification', and 'integration'.

Within the first process, an individual incorporates a regulation, though it has not been personalised as his own.[65] Motivation, therefore, arises from the external pressure to take the initiative to do something. Otherwise, an individual is subject to peer exclusion, which is an experience one wishes to avoid. Contingent self-esteem is the finest example of introjection.[66] Further, since it is based on the approval of others and social comparisons, one may well find similarities with the above-discussed concept of Social Identity Theory. Nonetheless, it is fallacious to make such a conclusion, given that *introjection* remains a 'controlled' form of internalised extrinsic motivation.

The second, identification, has an internal perceived locus of causality and is thus the opposite of introjection. The behaviour of a person under this motivation exhibits an aspect of himself that makes it, to some extent, authentic. Even though the activities are not intrinsically interesting, the subject feels a relative degree of freedom and volition, hence acknowledging the instrumental value of an action he needs to do.[67] Put differently, when an endeavour is perceived as relevant to one's life goals or is congruent with his interests, motivation automatically changes its locomotion towards autonomous behaviour.

Finally, integration is the most desirable process, in which people do what they are told to do without any form of external stimuli or supervision. It is an individual who willingly takes the initiative (hereby meaning 'motivates himself'), given the tremendous degree of self-congruence. As its name already suggests, the process of integration involves the incorporation of identification with one's true identity such that the behaviour emanates from the core of the subject's personality.[68] Despite sharing similarities with intrinsic motivation, integrated regulation still remains 'extrinsic' since the locomotion is done for the sake of perceived value. Not only does a person internalise the reason for an uninteresting activity but also appreciates the importance. To put it simply, a person is not interested in an activity, but it is the activity that itself is personally pivotal for life goals.

Inevitably, every activity could be intrinsically interesting, at least in theory, but this is an inaccurate lead. *Internalisation* is nothing short of a conceptual framework whereby an individual may adopt a behavioural pattern only by using this intelligence in practice. Usually, a subject approaches a tedious task because of the presence of external contingency.[69] Such involvement might allow the person to experience the activity's intrinsically interesting properties; hence, he could (but may not) develop through each level on a scale of motivation built on the previous experiences. Thus, in specific circumstances, people can integrate a new regulation with growing cognitive capacities, or they may lose that sense of instrumentality once the intrinsic factor of one's motivation diminishes.

As noted earlier, the type of motivation that drives a person to locomote in a specific way depends on the degree of volition an activity has. Calder and Staw[70] demonstrated that, under some conditions, an interaction occurs between intrinsic and extrinsic motivation. This seems to indicate that the self-perception of an individual determines whether or not a person would be more intrinsically or extrinsically motivated to buy a nostalgic product. This suggests that intrinsic motivation would exhibit the spontaneity and willingness of an individual to engage in shopping behaviour because of the inherent satisfaction indicative of 'impulse purchasing'. When the activity leads to an external outcome, in the current context of buying a nostalgic toy to meet a child's need, the underlying motivation is of an extrinsic character, as the purchase signifies a relationship between the actors engaged in the gift-giving social interaction.

Hedonic and utilitarian motivation

The role of consumption has undergone a dramatic shift. The growing recognition that the process of buying occurs not only for its most generic purpose, which is the act of purchase, but also for satisfying personal wants and needs, began in the 20th century when Dichter[71] endeavoured to comprehend the rising role of television and radio in developing consumerist patterns. Long until then, shopping had been concerned only with the product-oriented dimension, a desire to maximise utility. Specifically, society had not been of such a consumptive nature, meaning that every shopping activity was simply a utilitarian effort to obtain needed items at an affordable price. Had it not been for the notable enlargement of the working middle class, consumption would not have transformed to such an extent as it has today, and thus further investigations of drives behind specific purchase decisions would be useless whatsoever.[72] Nonetheless, a new dimension has emerged – one that does not limit consumption to simply product acquisition but also includes the complete experience. This notion served as a basis for a new framework, whereby shopping appears as a theme of work versus festive.[73]

Solomon[74] writes that people can be motivated to satisfy either utilitarian or hedonic needs. These exist under different terminology in different publications;[75] however, the fundamental idea is that customers deal with functional and non-functional shopping cues. Literature also recognises *social motivation*, which, similarly to Social Identity Theory (SIT), refers to the constant need to communicate and share experiences across individuals with resembling interests or belonging to the same group.[76]

Utilitarian motivation pertains to tangible aspects of products and their anticipated utility.[77] When an individual focuses on these rather practical needs, the literature emphasises that he behaves in a deliberate and efficient manner.[78] Teller et al.[79] indicated that 'efficiency' should be understood as a relationship between the purchase of a specific product (input) and efforts made by the consumer (output). Only after the successful accomplishment of the task, which is not necessarily the efficient purchase but also a collection of intelligence regarding the product alternatives through benchmarking, may the customer feel content. In opposition to the common prejudice that utilitarian motivation outlines independent personalities, research by Millan and Reynolds[80] indicated that such coherent behaviour portrays interdependent people.

That said, hedonic motivation is aesthetic, emotion-laden, and subjective. Hedonic consumption represents intangible entertainment and emotional worth. A 28-year-old male participant in a study by Fischer and Arnold[81] has accurately described hedonic consumer as 'a kid in a candy store', which means that his gratification would derive from immediate hedonic pleasure. The authors of the 1990 research have further indicated that the pursuit of such self-indulgent experiences matters more than the finalisation of the purchase. Moreover, these were male subjects who were more likely to justify their purchase in terms of hedonic values rather than practical ones.[82] Dhar and Wertenbroch[83] conducted a study to determine how utilitarian and hedonic motivations influence decision-making behaviour. It was revealed that in an approach-approach conflict situation where a person must choose between two desirable alternatives, hedonic products were the ones to be withdrawn first. In another study, Chandon et al.[84] provided evidence that when hedonic products are being advertised using analogous hedonic messages in the promotional campaigns, such products have higher premiums thereafter.

Hedonic consumers are intrinsically motivated ('shopping is fun'), whereas utilitarians are extrinsically motivated ('shopping feels like a mission'). Speaking about nostalgia, an intriguing characteristic of hedonic motivation is the anticipation of the pleasure a product provides. It is as if the individual enjoyed the product's benefits without buying it. Congruent with the concept of modern nostalgia, hedonic consumption may help deal with displeasing and sorrowful experiences from the past by confrontation via fantasy or emotional arousal.[85] Therefore, hedonic products are said to have higher premiums than utilitarian ones due to their promise of an increased self-worth they offer to the consumer.[86] This observation points to the fact that in a consistent manner, intrinsic and extrinsic forms of motivation interact with hedonic, utilitarian, and social motivation.

In the hedonic view, rather than being concerned with the completion of the task (shopping), consumers are playful and curiosity-driven; hence, they elicit pleasure from compulsory purchase activities as an emotional response resulting from the nostalgic effect. Hirschman and Holbrook[87] argued that hedonic consumers infuse a certain product with context-bound significance, dismantling it from the tangible attributes. This aspect invokes a carefree behaviour analogous to intrinsic motivation. Fischer and Arnold[88] found that males who acquired some Christmas gifts were more likely to manifest materialistic motives underlying the purchase. Utilitarian motivation may also be corresponding to the nostalgia-oriented purchases given the functional utilities of the product. When the subject of desire is so governing that an individual starts to construct the reality in an imaginative way, it seems logical that the purchase should be efficient and fast. Social motivation refers to the storytelling practices occurring within tribes as people seem to be influenced to buy a nostalgic product due to the communicated experience of others. In addition, the object of the purchase is believed to build and maintain social relations. Thus, the desire for nostalgic objects is social.

3.4 Chapter summary

The comprehensive analysis of social sciences literature emphasised the multifactorial nature of the notion of motivation, which has caused much confusion surrounding the concise meaning of the term. It is therefore conceded that 'motivation' is hardly a unitary phenomenon, given the fairly rapid evolution of ideas among the researchers. On the basis of Hull's[89] theory of 'anticipatory goal response', which directs an individual to locomote in a specific way, recent researchers[90] have endeavoured to emphasise the contemporaneity of the interrelated factors influencing human behaviour at a moment in time; hence, the emergence of dichotomous distinctions between orientations of motivation concerning the immediate determinants underlying a certain purposive behaviour, in this specific case, a nostalgic one indicative of a profoundly retrospective perspective of the current world.

The literature distinguishes intrinsic and extrinsic motivations as the most primal and closest to human nature; albeit, as discussed in the consumer-oriented perspective, research differentiates utilitarian and hedonic types of motivation. Embracing a perspective of nostalgia, the proposed framework suggests a hypothetical interaction between all the forms of motivations, consistent with the idea of 'personal causation'.[91] To be more precise, each type of motivation may significantly affect the consumer's inclination to acquire a nostalgic product due to the various attributes of the products being taken into consideration. However, which one will be the dominant catalysator of nostalgic behaviour will depend on personality factors. The authors suggest that intrinsically motivated consumers are presumed to engage in hedonic consumption activities, whereas those driven by extrinsically motivated behaviour will manifest an instrumental economic approach towards products.

Moreover, tribes offer only an ephemeral escape from the drudgeries of the present. Recent aspects of contemporary life involve paradoxes, namely the juxtaposition of seemingly contradictory themes: *individualism* (the search for one's self-actualisation) and *tribalism* (a quest to recompose social bonds), with the latter being the defining element of Western postmodernity, leading to a renewed interest in the search for authenticity.[92]

Overall, the desire of nostalgic consumers is felt to be a powerful emotion, making an individual indulge in dreamlike fantasies. Further, nostalgia was found to provide people with the perception that their lives are precious.[93] Belk et al.[94] pointed out that when people desire, they imaginatively construct 'an exciting world of wonder'. Such mental imagery overshadows utilitarian motives in the choice of product. Nostalgia, hereby defined as 'a preference toward objects that were common when one was younger', is just an emotional response to a stimulus, but what makes people behave in a specific way is to be found in the concomitants of their motivation.

Notes

1 Alba and Hasher, "Is Memory Schematic?", 203–231; Antonides and van Raaij, *Zachowanie konsumenta: Podręcznik akademicki*, 127.
2 Harrell, *Consumer Behavior*, 66.
3 Foxall and Goldsmith, *Psychologia konsumenta dla menedżera marketingu*, 69.
4 Antonides and van Raaij, *Zachowanie konsumenta: Podręcznik akademicki*, 132–136.
5 James, "Guilty through Association: Brand Association Transfer to Brand Alliances", 14–24.
6 Foxall and Goldsmith, *Psychologia konsumenta dla menedżera marketingu*, 119.
7 Solomon, *Zachowania i zwyczaje konsumentów*, 245–248.
8 Kessous and Roux, "Nostalgia, Autobiographical Memories, and Brand Communication: A Semiotic Analysis", 53–55.
9 Solomon et al., *Consumer Behaviour: A European Perspective*, 198.
10 Hamer, *Psychologia Społeczna: Teoria i Praktyka*, 125.
11 Antonides and van Raaij, *Zachowanie konsumenta: Podręcznik akademicki*, 183.
12 Lubiński, "The Effects of Nostalgia-Based Advertising on a Toy Company's Brand Equity: The Example of the LEGO Group", 32.
13 Atkinson, *An Introduction to Motivation*, 1–3.
14 Ryan and Deci, "Self-Determination Theory and the Facilitation of Intrinsic Motivation, Social Development, and Well-Being", 68.
15 Atkinson, *An Introduction to Motivation*, 4.
16 Atkinson, *An Introduction to Motivation*, 5.
17 Ryan and Deci, "Self-Determination Theory and the Facilitation of Intrinsic Motivation, Social Development, and Well-Being", 69.
18 James, *Text-Book of Psychology: Briefer Course*, 6.
19 Childers et al., "Hedonic and Utilitarian Motivations for Online Retail Shopping Behavior", 513.
20 Geuens et al., "An Exploratory Study of Grocery Shopping Motivations", 136.
21 Wahba and Bridwell, "Maslow Reconsidered: A Review of Research on the Need Hierarchy Theory", 213.
22 Alderfer, "An Empirical Test of a New Theory of Human Needs", 142.
23 Solomon et al., *Consumer Behaviour: A European Perspective*, 207.
24 Solomon et al., *Consumer Behaviour: A European Perspective*, 207.

25 Maddock, "A Theoretical and Empirical Substructure of Consumer Motivation and Behaviour".
26 Solomon et al., *Consumer Behaviour: A European Perspective*, 207.
27 Solomon et al., *Consumer Behaviour: A European Perspective*, 295.
28 Alderfer, "An Empirical Test of a New Theory of Human Needs", 143.
29 Shih, "VALS as a Tool of Tourism Market Research: The Pennsylvania Experience", 2–6.
30 Shih, "VALS as a Tool of Tourism Market Research: The Pennsylvania Experience", 2–6.
31 Solomon et al., *Consumer Behaviour: A European Perspective*, 221.
32 Shrum et al., "Individual Differences in Value Stability: Are We Really Tapping True Values?", n.p.
33 Shrum et al., "Individual Differences in Value Stability: Are We Really Tapping True Values?", n.p.
34 Kluckhohn, "Values and Value-Orientations in the Theory of Action: An Exploration in Definition and Classification", 395.
35 Atkinson, *An Introduction to Motivation*, 73–74.
36 Kluckhohn, "Values and Value-Orientations in the Theory of Action: An Exploration in Definition and Classification", 400.
37 Kluckhohn, "Values and Value-Orientations in the Theory of Action: An Exploration in Definition and Classification", 400.
38 Beatty et al., "Problems with VALS in International Marketing Research: An Example from an Application of the Empirical Mirror Technique", 376.
39 Solomon et al., *Consumer Behaviour: A European Perspective*, 222.
40 Kahle, "Alternative Measurement Approaches to Consumer Values: The List of Values (LOV) and Values and Life Style (VALS)", 406.
41 Beatty et al., "Problems with VALS in International Marketing Research: An Example from an Application of the Empirical Mirror Technique", 376.
42 Shrum et al., "Individual Differences in Value Stability: Are We Really Tapping True Values?", n.p.
43 Solomon and Buchanan, "A Role-Theoretic Approach to Product Symbolism: Mapping a Consumption Constellation", 95–109.
44 Veblen, *The Theory of the Leisure Class: An Economic Study of Institutions*, 96.
45 Solomon et al., *Consumer Behaviour: A European Perspective*, 221.
46 Authors note: The first VALS system divided people into 9 groups; the late VALS2 has slightly changed its segmentation, thus including 8 groups.
47 Solomon et al., *Consumer Behaviour: A European Perspective*, 222.
48 Mitchell, *The Nine American Life Styles*; Kahle, "Alternative Measurement Approaches to Consumer Values: The List of Values (LOV) and Values and Life Style (VALS)", 405–409.
49 Kahle, "Alternative Measurement Approaches to Consumer Values: The List of Values (LOV) and Values and Life Style (VALS)", 405.
50 Lawson and Todd, "Consumer Lifestyles: A Social Stratification Perspective", 297.

51 Callebaut et al., *Motivational Marketing Research Revisited.* Quoted in Poraj-Weder and Maison, "Poszukiwania uniwersalnego modelu motywacji konsumenckich", 25–26.
52 Solomon et al., *Consumer Behaviour: A European Perspective*, 199.
53 Childers et al., "Hedonic and Utilitarian Motivations for Online Retail Shopping Behavior", 513.
54 Solomon et al., *Consumer Behaviour: A European Perspective*, 201.
55 Gagné and Deci, "Self-Determination Theory and Work Motivation", 333–334.
56 Ryan and Deci, "Self-Determination Theory and the Facilitation of Intrinsic Motivation, Social Development, and Well-Being", 70.
57 Ryan and Deci, "Intrinsic and Extrinsic Motivations: Classic Definitions and New Directions", 58.
58 Ryan and Deci, "Intrinsic and Extrinsic Motivations: Classic Definitions and New Directions", 60.
59 Davis et al., "Extrinsic and Intrinsic Motivation to Use Computers in the Workplace", 1112.
60 Gagné and Deci, "Self-Determination Theory and Work Motivation", 331–362, 334.
61 Ryan and Deci, "Intrinsic and Extrinsic Motivations: Classic Definitions and New Directions", 61.
62 Davis et al., "Extrinsic and Intrinsic Motivation to Use Computers in the Workplace", 1114.
63 Ryan and Deci, "Intrinsic and Extrinsic Motivations: Classic Definitions and New Directions", 60–61.
64 Gagné and Deci, "Self-Determination Theory and Work Motivation", 334.
65 Ryan and Deci, "Intrinsic and Extrinsic Motivations: Classic Definitions and New Directions", 62.
66 Gagné and Deci, "Self-Determination Theory and Work Motivation", 334.
67 Ryan and Deci, "Self-Determination Theory and the Facilitation of Intrinsic Motivation, Social Development, and Well-Being", 73.
68 Gagné and Deci, "Self-Determination Theory and Work Motivation", 335.
69 Davis et al., "Extrinsic and Intrinsic Motivation to Use Computers in the Workplace", 1114.
70 Calder and Staw, "Self-Perception of Intrinsic and Extrinsic Motivation", 603–604.
71 Dichter, *The Strategy of Desire*, 51–52.
72 Vyse, "The Environment and Consumer Behaviour", 197–198.
73 Babin et al., "Work and/or Fun: Measuring Hedonic and Utilitarian Shopping Value", 644–656.
74 Solomon et al., *Consumer Behaviour: A European Perspective*, 202.
75 Tauber, "Why Do People Shop?" 46–49; Sheth, "Marketing Megatrends", 5–13; Westbrook and Black, "A Motivation-Based Shopper Typology", 78–103.
76 Geuens et al., "An Exploratory Study of Grocery Shopping Motivations", 136.
77 Geuens et al., "An Exploratory Study of Grocery Shopping Motivations", 136.

78 Childers et al., "Hedonic and Utilitarian Motivations for Online Retail Shopping Behavior", 513.
79 Teller et al., "Hedonic and Utilitarian Shopper Types in Evolved and Created Retail Agglomerations", 285.
80 Millan and Reynolds, "Self-Construals, Symbolic and Hedonic Preferences, and Actual Purchase Behavior", 558.
81 Fischer and Arnold, "More Than a Labor of Love: Gender Roles and Christmas Gift Shopping", 334.
82 Fischer and Arnold, "More Than a Labor of Love: Gender Roles and Christmas Gift Shopping", 334.
83 Dhar and Wertenbroch, "Consumer Choice between Hedonic and Utilitarian Goods", 775.
84 Chandon et al., "A Benefit Congruency Framework of Sales Promotion Effectiveness", 79.
85 Hirschman and Holbrook, "Hedonic Consumption: Emerging Concepts, Methods and Propositions", 96.
86 Solomon et al., *Consumer Behaviour: A European Perspective*, 202.
87 Hirschman and Holbrook, "Hedonic Consumption: Emerging Concepts, Methods and Propositions", 94.
88 Fischer and Arnold, "More than a Labor of Love: Gender Roles and Christmas Gift Shopping", 334.
89 Hull, "Goal Attraction and Directing Ideas Conceived as Habit Phenomena", 487–506.
90 Deci and Ryan, "The 'What' and 'Why' of Goal Pursuits: Human Needs and the Self-Determination of Behavior", 227–268; Childers et al., "Hedonic and Utilitarian Motivations for Online Retail Shopping Behavior", 511–535; Gagné and Deci, "Self-Determination Theory and Work Motivation", 331–362; Deci and Ryan, "Self-Determination Theory: A Macrotheory of Human Motivation, Development, and Health", 182–185.
91 de Charms, *Personal Causation: The Internal Affective Determinants of Behavior.*
92 Cova et al., "Rethinking Consumer Culture Theory from the Postmodern to the Communist Horizon", 214–215.
93 Routledge et al., "The Power of the Past: Nostalgia as a Meaning-Making Resource", 452–460.
94 Belk et al., "The Fire of Desire: A Multi-Sited Inquiry Into Consumer Passion", 333.

Reference list

Alba, Joseph W., and Lynn Hasher. "Is Memory Schematic?" *Psychological Bulletin* 93, no. 2 (1983): 203–231. https://doi.org/10.1037/0033-2909.93.2.203.

Alderfer, Clayton P. "An Empirical Test of a New Theory of Human Needs." *Organizational Behavior and Human Performance* 4, no. 1 (1969): 142–175. https://doi.org/10.1016/0030-5073(69)90004-X.

Antonides, Gerrit, and W. Fred van Raaij. *Zachowanie konsumenta: Podręcznik akademicki*. Warszawa: PWN, 2003.

Babin, Barry J., William R. Darden, and Mitch Griffin. "Work and/or Fun: Measuring Hedonic and Utilitarian Shopping Value." *Journal of Consumer Research* 20, no. 4 (1994): 644–656. https://doi.org/10.1086/209376.

Beatty, Sharon E., Pamela M. Homer, and Lynn R. Kahle. "Problems With VALS in International Marketing Research: An Example From an Application of the Empirical Mirror Technique." *Advances in Consumer Research* 16, no. 2 (1988): 375–380. https://doi.org/10.1177/0092070388016002.

Belk, Russell W., Güliz Ger, and Søren Askegaard. "The Fire of Desire: A Multisited Inquiry into Consumer Passion." *Journal of Consumer Research* 30, no. 3 (2003): 326–351. https://doi.org/10.1086/378613.

Calder, Bobby J., and Barry M. Staw. "Self-Perception of Intrinsic and Extrinsic Motivation." *Journal of Personality and Social Psychology* 31, no. 4 (1975): 599–605. https://doi.org/10.1037/h0077100.

Chandon, Pierre, Brian Wansink, and Gilles Laurent. "A Benefit Congruency Framework of Sales Promotion Effectiveness." *Journal of Marketing* 64, no. 4 (2000): 65–81. https://doi.org/10.1509/jmkg.64.4.65.18071.

Childers, Terry L., Christopher L. Carr, Joann Peck, and Stephen Carson. "Hedonic and Utilitarian Motivations for Online Retail Shopping Behavior." *Journal of Retailing* 77, no. 1 (2001): 511–535. https://doi.org/10.1016/S0022-4359(01)00056-2.

Cova, Bernard, Pauline Maclaran, and Alan Bradshaw. "Rethinking Consumer Culture Theory from the Postmodern to the Communist Horizon." *Marketing Theory* 13, no. 2 (2013): 213–225. https://doi.org/10.1177/1470593113477889.

Davis, Fred D., Richard P. Bagozzi, and Paul R. Warshaw. "Extrinsic and Intrinsic Motivation to Use Computers in the Workplace." *Journal of Applied Social Psychology* 22, no. 14 (1992): 1111–1132. https://doi.org/10.1111/j.1559-1816.1992.tb00945.x.

de Charms, Richard. *Personal Causation: The Internal Affective Determinants of Behavior*. 1st ed. New York: Routledge, 1983.

Deci, Edward L., and Richard M. Ryan. "Self-Determination Theory: A Macrotheory of Human Motivation, Development, and Health." *Canadian Psychology* 49, no. 3 (2008): 182–185. https://doi.org/10.1037/a0012801.

Deci, Edward L., and Richard M. Ryan. "The 'What' and 'Why' of Goal Pursuits: Human Needs and the Self-Determination of Behavior." *Psychological Inquiry* 11, no. 4 (2000): 227–268. https://doi.org/10.1207/S15327965PLI1104_01.

Dhar, Ravi, and Klaus Wertenbroch. "Consumer Choice Between Hedonic and Utilitarian Goods." *Journal of Marketing Research* 37, no. 1 (2000): 60–71. https://doi.org/10.1509/jmkr.37.1.60.18718.

Dichter, Ernest. *The Strategy of Desire*. Garden City, NY: Doubleday, 1960.

Fischer, Eileen, and Stephen J. Arnold. "More Than a Labor of Love: Gender Roles and Christmas Gift Shopping." *Journal of Consumer Research* 17, no. 3 (1990): 333–345. https://doi.org/10.1086/208561.

Foxall, Gordon R., and Ronald E. Goldsmith. *Psychologia konsumenta dla menedżera marketingu*. Warszawa: PWN, 1998.

Gagné, Marylène, and Edward L. Deci. "Self-Determination Theory and Work Motivation." *Journal of Organizational Behavior* 26, no. 4 (2005): 331–362. https://doi.org/10.1002/job.322.

Geuens, Maggie, Malaika Brengman, and Rosette S'Jegers. "An Exploratory Study of Grocery Shopping Motivations." *European Advances in Consumer Research* 5, no. 1 (2001): 135–140.

Hamer, Hanna. *Psychologia Społeczna: Teoria i Praktyka*. Warsaw, Poland: Difin, 2005.

Harrell, Gilbert. *Consumer Behavior*. San Diego: Harcourt Brace Jovanovich, 1986.

Hirschman, Elizabeth C., and Morris B. Holbrook. "Hedonic Consumption: Emerging Concepts, Methods and Propositions." *Journal of Marketing* 46, no. 3 (1982): 92–101. https://doi.org/10.1177/002224298204600314.

Hull, Clark L. "Goal Attraction and Directing Ideas Conceived as Habit Phenomena." *Psychological Review* 38, no. 6 (1931): 487–506. https://doi.org/10.1037/h0071442.

James, David. "Guilty through Association: Brand Association Transfer to Brand Alliances." *Journal of Consumer Marketing* 22, no. 1 (2005): 14–24. https://doi.org/10.1108/07363760510576518.

James, William. *Text-Book of Psychology: Briefer Course*. New York: Henry Holt, 1892.

Kahle, Lynn R., Sharon E. Beatty, and Pamela Homer. "Alternative Measurement Approaches to Consumer Values: The List of Values (LOV) and Values and Life Style (VALS)." *Journal of Consumer Research* 13, no. 3 (1986): 405–409. https://doi.org/10.1086/209079.

Kessous, Aurelie, and Elyette Roux. "Nostalgia, Autobiographical Memories, and Brand Communication: A Semiotic Analysis." *Marketing ZFP* 35, no. 1 (2013): 50–57. https://doi.org/10.15358/0344-1369_2013_1_50.

Kluckhohn, Clyde. "Values and Value-Orientations in the Theory of Action: An Exploration in Definition and Classification." In *Toward a General Theory of Action*, edited by Talcott Parsons and Edward A. Shils, 388–433. Cambridge, MA: Harvard University Press, 1951.

Lawson, Rob A., and Sarah L. Todd. "Consumer Lifestyles: A Social Stratification Perspective." *Marketing Theory* 2, no. 3 (2002): 295–307. https://doi.org/10.1177/147059310200200327.

Lubiński, Kamil. "The Effects of Nostalgia-Based Advertising on a Toy Company's Brand Equity: The Example of the LEGO Group." *Zeszyty Naukowe Uniwersytetu Ekonomicznego w Krakowie* 6, no. 990 (2020): 29–48. https://doi.org/10.15678/ZNUEK.2020.0990.0602.

Maddock, Richard. "A Theoretical and Empirical Substructure of Consumer Motivation and Behaviour." In *European Advances in Consumer Research*, edited by Flemming Hansen, 29–37. Provo, UT: Association for Consumer Research, 1995.

Millan, Elena, and Jonathan Reynolds. "Self-Construals, Symbolic and Hedonic Preferences, and Actual Purchase Behavior." *Journal of Retailing and Consumer Services* 21, no. 4 (2014): 550–560. https://doi.org/10.1016/j.jretconser.2014.03.012.

Mitchell, Arnold. *The Nine American Life Styles*. New York: MacMillan Publishing, 1983.

Poraj-Weder Magdalena, and Dominika Maison. "Poszukiwania uniwersalnego modelu motywacji konsumenckich." *Psychologia Społeczna* 1, no. 32 (2015): 24–35. https://doi.org/10.7366/1896180020153202.

Routledge, Clay, Tim Wildschut, Constantine Sedikides, Jacob Juhl, and Jamie Arndt. "The Power of the Past: Nostalgia as a Meaning-Making Resource." *Memory* 20, no. 5 (2012): 452–460. https://doi.org/10.1080/09658211.2012.677452.

Ryan, Richard M., and Edward L. Deci. "Intrinsic and Extrinsic Motivations: Classic Definitions and New Directions." *Contemporary Educational Psychology* 25, no. 1 (2000): 54–67. https://doi.org/10.1006/ceps.1999.1020.

Ryan, Richard M., and Edward L. Deci. "Self-Determination Theory and the Facilitation of Intrinsic Motivation, Social Development, and Well-Being." *American Psychologist* 55, no. 1 (2000): 68–78. https://doi.org/10.1037/0003-066X.55.1.68.

Sheth, Jagdish N. "Marketing Megatrends." *Journal of Consumer Marketing* 1, no. 1 (1983): 5–13. https://doi.org/10.1108/eb008078.

Shih, David. "VALS as a Tool of Tourism Market Research: The Pennsylvania Experience." *Journal of Travel Research* 24, no. 4 (1986): 2–6. https://doi.org/10.1177/004728758602400404.

Shrum, L. J., John A. Mccarty, and Tamara L. Loeffler. "Individual Differences in Value Stability: Are We Really Tapping True Values?" *ACR North American Advances* (1990): n.p.

Solomon, Michael R. *Zachowania i zwyczaje konsumentów*. Gliwice: Helion, 2006.

Solomon, Michael R., and Bruce Buchanan. "A Role-Theoretic Approach to Product Symbolism: Mapping a Consumption Constellation." *Journal of Business Research* 22, no. 1 (1991): 95–109. https://doi.org/10.1016/0148-2963(91)90044-X.

Solomon, Michael R., Gary J. Bamossy, Soren Askegaard, and Margaret K. Hogg. *Consumer Behaviour: A European Perspective*. 6th ed. United Kingdom: Pearson Education Limited, 2016.

Tauber, Edward M. "Why Do People Shop?" *Journal of Marketing* 36, no. 4 (1972): 46–49. https://doi.org/10.1177/002224297203600409.

Teller, Christoph, Thomas Reutterer, and Peter Schnedlitz. "Hedonic and Utilitarian Shopper Types in Evolved and Created Retail Agglomerations." *The International Review of Retail, Distribution and Consumer Research* 18, no. 3 (2008): 283–309. https://doi.org/10.1080/09593960802113877.

Vyse, Stuart. "The Environment and Consumer Behaviour." In *Environmental Psychology and Human Well-Being*, edited by Ann Sloan Devlin, 193–220. 1st ed. Elsevier Inc., 2018. https://doi.org/10.1016/B978-0-12-811481-0.00008-1.

Wahba, Mahmoud A., and Lawrence G. Bridwell. "Maslow Reconsidered: A Review of Research on the Need Hierarchy Theory." *Organizational Behavior and Human Performance* 15, no. 2 (1976): 212–240. https://doi.org/10.1016/0030-5073(76)90038-6.

Westbrook, Robert A., and William C. Black. "A Motivation-Based Shopper Typology." *Journal of Retailing* 61, no. 1 (1985): 78–103.

Part II

Nostalgic branding in toy industry – research results

Introduction to Part II

Due to the lack of sufficient data on the impact of nostalgia on consumer attitudes and behaviour in the process of purchasing toys and the absence of studies addressing the positioning of nostalgic brands in the toy industry, empirical research was conducted. This research involved two stages focusing on the impact of nostalgia on brand positioning in the toy industry, particularly in the context of nostalgic brand perception and consumer motivations.

The first stage consisted of qualitative research using projective techniques and group in-depth interviews with focus groups. As this monograph is rooted in the meaning-based tradition of research, the authors adopted an interpretive framework suitable for focus group studies. The research was conducted among 72 consumers representing generations X, Y, and Z during the second and fourth quarters of 2022 in Poland. The analyses aimed to determine consumer attitudes towards nostalgic toy brands, their motivations for purchase, and the key factors influencing the image of these brands.

The second stage involved quantitative research using indirect communication methods with respondents (consumers) through a structured questionnaire. The study utilised the Computer-Assisted Web Interviewing (CAWI) technique with an online self-administered questionnaire and the Paper and Pencil Interview (PAPI) technique with a self-administered paper questionnaire. The survey was conducted in the first quarter of 2023. The sample included three demographic cohorts: Generation X, Millennials, and Generation Z, with 535 completed survey questionnaires collected.

The results of both research stages are presented in this section of the monograph to support the assertion that nostalgia can be effectively leveraged by toy companies to strengthen brand perception.

This part also integrates existing research on brand positioning with the findings from both qualitative and quantitative studies. The results provide valuable insights, responding to recent demands for further exploration of

DOI: 10.4324/9781003606079-6

the connection between nostalgic positioning and consumers' emotional responses to products. Furthermore, the authors offer practical recommendations for crafting impactful brand positioning strategies in the toy industry, based on the study's findings.

4 Perception of nostalgic brands in toy industry – results of a qualitative study

4.1 Research aims and methods

For the purpose of this monograph, apart from the literature review performed with the use of the method of literature analysis and review, as well as systematic literature review, the authors have conducted their own empirical research based on the concept of triangulation, whose aim is the evaluation of the impact of nostalgia on consumer attitudes and nostalgia-oriented purchases in the context of consumers' motivations, as exemplified in the toy industry, to assess finally toys' nostalgic brand positioning. Data collection was conducted via various methods, which has been followed by comparing and combining the results. In the practical part, two stages of research were performed that were mentioned in the Introduction and are described thoroughly in the consecutive parts of the monograph.

The research procedure was conducted according to the diagram depicted in Figure 4.1.

As a result of the in-depth literature review, a deficiency in publications on the positioning of nostalgic brands in the toy industry has been observed, identifying a theoretical-empirical gap in this field. In order to fill in this gap, the profile of consumers has been identified. Due to the specificity of the toy sector, consumers representing X, Y, and Z generations were selected as people who purchase toys for their own children as presents or to satisfy their own needs.

There seem to be some disagreements regarding the dates used to describe the demographic characteristics of the consumers representing a particular age cohort.[1] In the domestic and foreign literature, discussion is ongoing about the age ranges to identify the specific market segment. The present monograph adopts the following definitions for each generation: X (1965–1980), Y (1981–1996), and Z (1997–2012).

It is worth stressing that the representatives of these generations in particular are the first in Poland who have memories related to the popular toy brands.

DOI: 10.4324/9781003606079-7

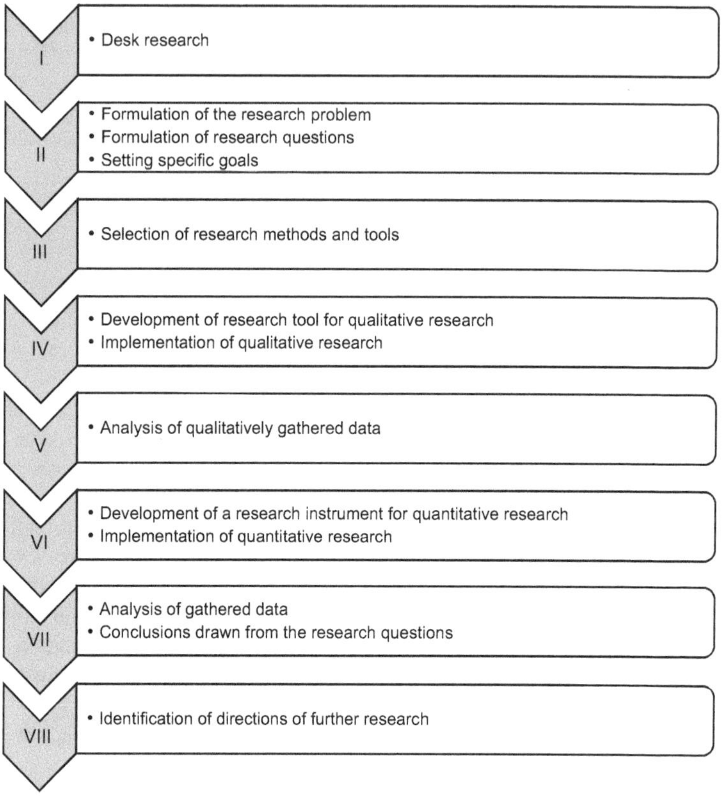

Figure 4.1 The research procedure

On the basis of the literature review and taking the subject of research into account, the following research questions were formulated:

Q1: What are the brands of nostalgic toys characteristic for representatives of generations X, Y, and Z?

Q2: What are the attitudes of consumers – representing particular generations – towards toy brands? Do consumers show nostalgic attitudes towards toy brands known from childhood?

Q3: What factors influence the purchase of a toy from a nostalgic brand?

Q4: What types of motivation influence the purchase of a toy from nostalgic brand for yourself and as a gift for a child?

Q5: Do nostalgic attitudes influence the purchase of toys?

Q6: How to perform positioning of a nostalgic brand in the toy industry?

Next, research methods and tools were selected. In order to ensure a high quality of analyses, the authors decided to use the triangulation method. Its implementation has allowed for the use of quantitative and qualitative methods. The study was divided into two stages.

The first stage entailed qualitative research using group-in-depth interviews and projecting techniques on the focus groups. The research was conducted among consumers representing X, Y, and Z generations in the second and fourth quarters of 2022. The analyses were performed to determine consumer attitudes towards toy brands, their motivation to buy and to identify the key factors affecting the image of these brands. The methodology and research results were described thoroughly in the subsequent sections of this chapter. The results of qualitative analyses have enabled answering selected research questions as well as creating tools for the main quantitative study.

In the second stage of research, quantitative analyses based on the method of indirect communication with respondents (consumers), using a questionnaire, were performed. The scrutiny was performed in the first quarter of 2023. The methodology and research results of the quantitative study were described thoroughly in Chapter 4.

The obtained research results were statistically handled, and relevant analyses were performed. As a result, conclusions were formulated, and the directions for further research were outlined.

4.2 Methodology of the qualitative research

To take up the method of interpretive research, the authors opted to employ focus groups using group-in-depth interviews and projecting techniques. The wide acceptance of the method in the marketing literature dates back to motivation research in the 1950s.[2] Social sciences, however, had to wait until the 1980s, when the research technique was borrowed from marketing practices of conducting 'group in-depth interviews'[3] that posit that the social interaction between participatory subjects yields qualitative data.[4] In this light, 'focus groups' is an umbrella term that encapsulates the technique's ability to encourage participation in discussion, elicit participants' depth accounts, and release inhibitions that might preclude individuals from unveiling further details.[5]

As opposed to individual structured interviews, as noted by Kitzinger,[6] focus groups have the strength that they manage to retrieve information from subjects reluctant to participate in one-on-one meetings. It is thus a disclosive practice allowing participants to engage in an informal discussion making visible all the aspects of the psychological environment that have not been revealed before.[7] Much of the behaviour is overdetermined by subliminal stimuli, of which profound motives are concealed in a typical interpersonal interaction. The group-interview technique is concerned with uncovering these unconscious motives since these lead to self-disclosure, which Jourard[8] had poetically portrayed as 'the portal to the human soul'. In no way is this subjective side of man disclosed more than through an individual's willingness to make his self-concept known. Once the subject finds himself in comfortable surroundings, he manifests his true self. The distinctive feature of focus groups lies in the researcher's endeavour to imitate the delineated 'natural setting' in which interactions of contemporaneous influences occur between humans.[9] Therefore, the more socially oriented the field is, the more relevant and valid the data becomes. Nevertheless, to make sure that the subjects' disclosures convey a sense of childish spontaneity, untainted by the dissemblance manifested in the individual's intrinsic escape from the unpleasantness of being humiliated,[10] such groups ought to be 'cohesive' in the way that the participants share a common identity relevant to the focus of the group interview.[11] Specifically, individuals seem to be predisposed to divulge more details about themselves to people who share commonalities in their worldviews.[12] Self-disclosure entails boldness, and such can be mustered exclusively through overt interactions with another human being. The researcher's responsibility, then, is to foster natural spontaneity, no matter how embarrassing the submitted ideas might be, so as to avert behavioural duplicity, and this can be done by establishing homogeneity in the group.[13] As Krueger[14] summarises, the researcher should strive 'to create a comfortable, permissive environment to focus groups'. Consistent with the ontological assumptions of the dynamically changing world, focus groups defy individuals to hold views unless there is a change of heart after listening to others. Henceforth, Morgan[15] concludes that achieving consensus is not requisite for the validity of the research, given the serendipitous influences of qualitative underpinnings. The research question and design of the study, as remarked by Doody et al.,[16] ultimately inform the conduct of the focus group.

The final characteristic of focus groups is that the researcher is the primary instrument, as he is directly involved in the substance of the conversation by moderating its process.[17] That is, a researcher may immediately clarify what poses constraints on the way the participants understand the investigated phenomenon. As a moderator, to probe qualitative information, the researcher must develop a coherent rapport with participatory subjects, know when to hamper a chatty group, engage the reluctant ones to share their thought, and, above all, the authors must sustain the focus of the discussion to revolve around the relevant topic, as Morgan[18] contends. It follows, therefore, that the researcher's proficiency in moderating the interview affects the reliability and validity of the findings.[19]

Since constructivism posits that one's developed understanding of the world is a direct consequence of a past experience, the focus group is a retrospective analysis emphasising a 'particular concrete situation'.[20] The goals of this research, then, were to obtain a holistic understanding based on the social context – the cultural setting in which the data collection takes place, that is, identification and evaluations of the impact of nostalgia on consumer attitudes and purchase behaviours in the context of consumers' motivations, as well as evaluation of the impact of nostalgia on brand image in the toy industry. By acknowledging contemporaneous influences, which comprise the strength of a tendency towards specific behaviour, the researcher contributes a unique depiction of what he has learnt about the phenomenon through the lens of group behaviour.[21]

The study by Sierra and McQuitty[22] was the first to rely on Social Identity Theory assumption, whereby being a member of a collective entity at some time in the past provokes a change in behaviour once the stimulus corresponding to that time period arises. In other words, cognitive and emotional factors simultaneously impact decisions regarding purchasing nostalgia-induced products. Regrettably, the rhetoric of the study is expressed in the quantitative language of numbers and models, unable to provide a detailed description of emotions. Therefore, the authors of the following monograph chose focus groups with the combined use of a choice experiment to produce an in-depth depiction of motifs expressed in nostalgic consumption behaviour, for quantitative measures, and the statistical analyses did not develop a complex picture of the phenomenon. First, the study sought to confirm whether or not there is a significant difference in purchase intentions for nostalgic versus non-nostalgic toy products in a forced-choice experiment. Second, it examined consumers' attitudes towards focal nostalgic toy brands. Third, it delivered a densely structured description of the nostalgia phenomenon, as conveyed in subjects' depth accounts, and elucidated how it did manifest. Finally, by bearing the stamp of the experiment, embedded in the roots of projective techniques, the study has contributed an appropriate and accessible tool to facilitate self-disclosure that may be otherwise challenging to unveil.

Since the following monograph has its roots in the meaning-based tradition of research, the authors adapted an interpretive framework that is achievable in focus groups. Stewart et al.[23] argue that many focus groups in the fields of sociology, psychology, and marketing gather individuals with a commonality of purpose and identity. Sharing a common interest is an antecedent of establishing the group's cohesiveness.[24] Once composed, a group forms a theoretically meaningful population and hence underscores the research's reliability. When participants have something in common, this commonality must be germane to the themes imposed by a researcher. Indeed, the participants were purposively sampled on the basis of the commonality of their demographic cohort (as presented in Table 4.1).

A total of 72 participants representing generations X, Y, and Z attended a series of focus groups. Six focus group discussions were conducted at the Lodz University of Technology in Lodz, Poland, in the period from April to November 2022. In each focus group, eight to 18 people participated, all of whom were consumers who purchased toys for their own children as presents or to satisfy their own individual needs. Knowledge of the six focal brands chosen for the purpose of this study (of which profiles are delineated

Table 4.1 Overview of focus group participants

Generation X		*Generation Y*		*Generation Z*	
1965–1980		1980–1996		1997+	
Males	Females	Males	Females	Males	Females
7	10	14	9	12	20
Two meetings in October and November 2022		Two meetings in April 2022		Two meetings in May 2022	

in Table 3.4) was not a prerequisite for the participants' selection. The participants' ages ranged from 18 to 58 years to ensure the representation of each of the three focal demographic cohorts. The group profiles included university employees (two groups) and university students (four groups). All of the focus groups, which lasted for an hour and a half each, were moderated by the authors of the monograph themselves in a non-directive, self-managed fashion to encourage a relaxed flow of discussion. The authors' involvement in probing for information was minimal to evade the disaffection of a participant, who would misinterpret such pursuits as putting pressure on them, thereby limiting further engagement, as recommended by Bray et al.[25] By prior agreement, all focus groups were audio recorded on smartphone, transcribed verbatim, and thematically analysed. To ensure anonymity, no names or other identifiers of the participatory subjects were used.

Participants were presented with sets of images depicting three toys being offered by specific brands. Though overlooked and deemed elusive, pictorial representations incorporate qualitative power in stimulating ideas regarding the topic under discussion.[26]

Each image cluster included three different variants of the toy:

- a nostalgic new one referring to the past,
- a current one,
- a nostalgic old one from the past.

The selection of toy brands derived from the report of worldwide revenue within the industry in 2021 (Table 4.2).

Since one of the central themes surrounding nostalgia is 'event' (hereby understood as 'special occasions'), and gifts were identified to be the kind of material possessions a child regards as 'special',[28] the choice experiment aimed to reconstruct the activity of browsing through toy catalogues. The authors of this monograph intended to embrace the possibilities of pictorial representations to invoke nostalgia-laden memories in participants, given that photographs can indeed produce nostalgia.[29] The order of images had no effect on the results of the study and is therefore not discussed further.

Table 4.2 Focal toy manufacturers chosen for the study based on global revenue in 2021 *based on the data obtained from statista.com.*[27]

Company	*Foundation date*	*Applied nostalgic strategy*	*Global revenue (in million US dollars)*
LEGO	1934	Generational	8,419.62
Bandai	1950	Transgenerational	7,292.01
Hasbro	1923	Transgenerational	6,420.4
Mattel	1945	Generational	5,457.7

After viewing the focal toy products, the subjects participated in group in-depth interviews regarding the remembrance of childhood in the context of their social group membership. The authors have consciously refrained from using the word 'nostalgia' throughout the focus groups, trying to rely as much on the group member's knowledge of the phenomenon as possible. Specifically, the authors asked the participants to describe a toy they had enjoyed playing with during childhood. It was foreseen that within a permissive, comfortable environment, the subjects' self-disclosures would ultimately lead to the verbalisation of the nostalgic feeling. Following a general topic, the content of the discussion moved on to whether or not the toy they have just declared to be their favourite object of play was a golden ticket to affiliation with attractive social groups – a collection of individuals in which an individual assumes immense similarity with other members of the tribe. As the focus group sessions progressed and themes emerged, participants were then asked if they had ever purchased a nostalgia-themed toy. If the response was negative or the participants were reluctant to speak on this, an additional question was posed asking, '[w]hen it comes to your relatives, do you base your toy-buying decision on your interests?'.

Finally, participants were presented with images of logos of the six toy brands (Table 4.3). In support of the proposal of Muehling et al.[31] that exposure to nostalgia-themed products along with one's propensity to walk down memory lanes is more likely to produce more favourable brand attitudes, the participants were to conjure associations with the displayed brand logos. These responses were utilised to build the consumers' perception of each brand in the form of a word cloud.

4.3 Nostalgic perception of chosen toy brands – results of the qualitative research

The structure of each subsection presenting the results of research for individual brands includes

- presentation of toy options for different generations;
- discussion of the choices made by representatives of particular generations;

Table 4.3 Profiles of focal toy brands

Brand name	*Toy licensee(s)*	*Type of asset*	*Targeted audience*	*Appropriate age*
Barbie	Mattel, Mega Brands	Original toy line	Girls	3+
LEGO	LEGO	Original toy line	Unisex	4–99 years
My Little Pony	Hasbro	Original toy line and media franchise	Girls	3–8 years
Pokémon	Bandai, Hasbro, Mattel, The Pokémon Company, Takara Tomy	Licence and media franchise	Unisex	4+
Power Rangers	Bandai, Hasbro	Licence	Boys	4+
Transformers	Bandai, Hasbro, LEGO.[30] Takara Tomy	Original toy line and media franchise	Boys	6+

- discussion of associations related to a given brand in the context of nostalgic attitudes and Social Identity Theory;
- word cloud reflecting the participant's perception of the chosen brand.

The findings from group in-depth interviews, of which content included general memories and purchases of toys, are also presented.

Nostalgic perception of Power Rangers brand

Generation X participants were presented with three images representing the Power Rangers-themed toy line, each representing seemingly different variants of the product. These included the following:

A Power Rangers Lightning Collection Wild Force Lunar Wolf Ranger Figure (*a nostalgic new one referring to the past*);
B Power Rangers Mighty Morphin Jason Red Ranger Figure (*a nostalgic old one from the past*);
C Power Rangers Dino Fury Black Ranger with Shield Sleeve (*a current one*).

Xers, as further discussion would reveal, seemed to have no cognisance of the show. One of the constraints was the identification of trends in toy purchasing, as the people in the X generation were nearly equally divided between the three options. Regardless, there seemed to be a propensity to purchase 'the present variant of the toy' (the autumn 2022 action figure), presumably, as the safe pick. Few individuals would fancy the 1993 Red Ranger figure.

The nostalgic variant was the least popular choice, and, in particular, those were the youngest participants from the X generation who would make such a decision. This corroborated the earlier findings, whereby a brand in no way is able to stimulate consumers' maudlin responses without preceding past exposure and attachment to the brand. While displaying the images, a female participant in the X generation stated that the depicted action figures look '*odd and bizarre*'.

Generation Y participants were presented with three images representing the Power Rangers-themed toy line, each representing seemingly different variants of the product. These included the following:

A Power Rangers Mighty Morphin Deluxe Set Megazord (*a nostalgic old one from the past*)
B Power Rangers Dino Fury Green Ranger with Sprint Sleeve (*a current one*)
C Power Rangers Lightning Collection Mighty Morphin Red Ranger Figure (*a nostalgic new one referring to the past*)

What immediately struck the authors was that the new nostalgic variant was twice as popular as the present variant of a toy. Indeed, the 'Lightning Collection' toyline, whose figure of the Red Ranger is instantiated, was introduced to target Millennials. However, because they appeared to be the least talkative subjects of all examined cohorts, it remained unclear whether it was the alleged exposure to the show that elicited a behavioural response from Ys that was associated with the merchandise. Paradoxically, not a single individual, unlike post-Millennials, was willing to admit that he has watched the show regularly, presumably due to the negative connotations surrounding the clichéd storyline or occasional lack thereof. Dino Fury Green Ranger was the second most wanted toy, with the 1993 Megazord (nostalgic old one), probably one of the most sought-after toys of the 1990s, being only the third.

Generation Z participants were presented with three images representing the Power Rangers-themed toy line, each representing seemingly different variants of the product. These included the following:

A Power Rangers Lightning Collection S.P.D. Shadow Ranger Figure *(a nostalgic new one referring to the past)*
B Power Rangers Mystic Force Knight Wolf to Dark Fury Dragon Figure *(a nostalgic old one from the past)*
C Power Rangers Dino Fury Green Ranger with Sprint Sleeve *(a current one)*

It seems that the authors must have perfectly adapted the stimuli to the participatory subjects, for the vast majority of the post-Millennials have enthusiastically opted for the nostalgic variant of the Power Rangers figure referring to the *Space Patrol Delta* show aired in 2005. In the words of one participant: '*You [the authors] have no idea how prodigious memories these images have just awakened. [Memoirs] of a toy I once had and have forgotten about its existence, until this very moment*'. Due to the sentiment towards the show, he unhesitatingly elected the collector's rendition. And so did the preponderance of the participants. The passion with which he spoke about it contrasts markedly with what the authors observed in Millennials, endeavouring to conceal the fact they have watched the show at any cost. The Knight Wolf Figure, which was the old variant of the toy, taken from the *Mystic Force*-themed toyline, was the second choice. Only one man would consider purchasing the present variant of a toy.

The authors asked the participants the following question: '*What is the first word that comes to your mind when seeing the displayed logo?*'. Walter Benjamin, whose name is often invoked in Brown's works,[32] argued that nostalgia is where a paradox is. Conceptualised as 'antimony',[33] a paradox allows consumers to devote emotionally to the co-creation of a brand's value, thereby expropriating the company from its onus of attributing it to the merchandise. Indeed, the word cloud of Power Rangers' associations reflected a paradoxical essence, a 'paradessence', to the same degree as the franchise brand appears. Damned by critics and salespersons for being a little over the top, while being enamoured by kids and audiences for the superhero-ish crux of the storyline, Power Rangers, similarly to LEGO's Bionicle, has found its special ingredient to success in its own right.

At first glance, the participants conjured impressions attributed to the notion of uber-masculinity, such as 'power', 'strength', or 'might', with the latter failing to materialise, however. On the downside, a group of Ys

Figure 4.2 Word cloud reflecting the participant's perception of 'Power Rangers'

seemed to be more reflective on the condemnatory dismay revolving around the themes of 'puerility', 'cliché', and 'stupid'. Still on the subject of the Millennial generation is another paradox, for the word cloud indicates lots of references to the introductory season of the show, '*Mighty Morphin Power Rangers*', the watching of which made most of the participants feel humiliated, as hinted at earlier in the first part of the study, where they seemed to refrain from making comments on why they had chosen a particular Ranger figurine. This behavioural trend became particularly apparent throughout the discussion part. Words carrying negative connotations of disdain might well be a defensive reaction against disclosing innately fragile pieces of an inner child, for if closely examined, the participants' perception of the franchise brand shall evoke an image of one's carefree childhood spent watching *Power Rangers* that ran on Saturday mornings. It feels as if these associations have been used to conceal the implicit meaning that could be discerned only when arranged together. In this regard, watching *Power Rangers* might be considered an intimate experience, conveying maudlin sentimentality towards childhood. As one of the males in Gen Y has finally revealed, '*[i]t is always astonishing to see a giant robot engaged in overscaled combat sequences fighting a monster. Take "Pacific Rim" [a 2013 film], for example*'. There is an incongruity to it all, though, as post-Millennial participants, in stark contrast, not only were they the most engaged of all groups, but most noticeably, they felt confident to talk about Power Rangers, highlighting their favourite seasons.

Nostalgic perception of Barbie brand

Generation X participants were presented with three images representing the Barbie-themed toy line, each representing seemingly different variants of the product:

A Barbie Holiday Doll *(a current one)*;
B Barbie Entrepreneur *(a nostalgic old one from the past)*;
C Barbie Superstar *(a nostalgic new one referring to the past)*.

The 2022 Barbie Holiday Doll was the most commonly chosen variant of the toy. All male subjects were inclined to favour the present variant in the wake of the doll's glaring newness, among other alternatives. Females' decisions, on the other hand, seemed to have been influenced by criteria such as accessories, outfits, or hairstyles. Taken all in all, the apparent common denominator for both genders was the doll's exquisite red dress. It is hence likely that the more astounding a piece of needlecraft a toy has, the more the possibility of purchasing it when urged to do so. Two participants opted for the old variant of the doll (1984 Barbie Entrepreneur aka Day-to-Night), of which one confessed to having owned this doll. An immediate nostalgic reaction was observed as the participant shared a personal story of how she became the owner of her Barbie. Only a single individual chose the new nostalgic variant.

Generation Y participants were presented with three images representing the Barbie-themed toy line, each representing seemingly different variants of the product:

A 2014 Barbie Entrepreneur *(a nostalgic new one referring to the past)*;
B Barbie with Short Blue Sequins Mini Dress *(a current one)*;
C 1984 Barbie Entrepreneur aka Day-to-Night *(a nostalgic old one from the past)*.

The vast majority of Millennials were opting for the present variant, as happened among people from the X generation. Females, it should be emphasised, were outnumbered by males in the Y cohort. Given this relative disproportion, it is therefore tempting to conclude that once a consumer approaches a product offered under a brand name unbeknownst to him, which in this example is addressing girls, he shall unconsciously elect the most current version of the product. Secondly, one could espy a recurring decision-making pattern based on the doll's outfit. Although the toy differed vastly from the one displayed to Xers, there was nothing that would inhibit Generation Y from picking superficially the same 'contemporary variant'. It appears that all the components that constitute the visual reception can be determinative of whether or not to buy a product. Sequins, slender shapes, and a contrast of colours – these may be the details intended to seize the consumer's attention. Just a few people in Generation Y expressed a desire to buy the nostalgic toy. Finally, nobody was interested in buying the classic version of the Barbie doll ('Barbie Entrepreneur').

Generation Z participants were presented with three images representing the Barbie-themed toy line, each representing seemingly different variants of the product:

A 2005 Barbie Fashion Fever Modern Trends Collection Doll *(a nostalgic old one from the past)*;
B Toy Story 4-themed Barbie *(a nostalgic new one referring to the past)*;
C 2014 Barbie Entrepreneur *(a current one)*.

Barbie Entrepreneur, which served as a nostalgic stimulus for Generation Y, in this case, was assigned a new role as the contemporary toy. And it was this variant of the toy that enjoyed its popularity among post-Millennials. Zs were also more likely to prefer the nostalgic variant (possibly triggered by the reference to Disney's *Toy Story* franchise, although the doll itself evokes the 1983 Great Shape Barbie, later known as Working Out Barbie in 1996), while the rest of the participants chose the old version of the toy, which entails a situation whereby a person would have reclaimed the object of the once unsatisfied past, had it been possible. Among other observations, the authors noticed that Barbie was specifically the only toy brand that made Zs chuckle.

The authors asked the participants the following question: '*What is the first word that comes to your mind when seeing the displayed logo?*'. The association that figured out most prominently during focus groups was the name of the plastic doll: 'Barbie', '*in full Barbara*', as one of the participants remarked. Understandably, it would be impossible to overlook Ken, the doll's presumed lifelong partner, who has been accompanying her since 1961 when he got introduced as 'Barbie's ultimate accessory'. And so, one participant intimately associated Barbie with her 'grandma', who had single-handedly been knitting the doll's '*beautifully crafted dresses on a machine*'. As she revealed, '*back then [at some point in the 1980s], accessories were incredibly steep and inaccessible*'. Therefore, since grandma was a proficient tailor, the needlecraft of the apparel appeared not as formidable as it would have seemed. Continuing in this vein, another female participant, this time among post-Millennials, brought evocative reflections related to her father, who had once carpentered a wooden 'dollhouse'.

The third participant, in turn, shared a rich-in-memories story from her childhood where 'dreams do come true'. As she reminisced,

> *One summer, I visited my aunt who lived in a coastal city in France. Every day when we were coming back from the beach with my mum, I had been popping into the tiny toy store on the way home.*

The store, as she continued, was filled with '*a wealth of toys I had never seen in Poland*'. Among the many wonders therein, the one that had drawn particular attention was the 'Barbie Entrepreneur' doll with a full range of

Figure 4.3 Word cloud reflecting the participant's perception of 'Barbie'

accessories. She had been thinking about it, dreaming that one day this charming figurine would be hers, regardless of what her mum said. And it was at this moment that the aunt gave her the doll as a gift, thereby realising a dream that she had long indulged in.

All these stories circle around the idea of Barbie's perceived expensiveness; hence, the materialisation of 'steep' in the word cloud. This is also evident in another association, 'sold separately' – a recurring disclosure heard at the end of the commercials. It is important to note that among associations to the word 'Barbie', some (e.g., 'catfish', 'plastic', 'skinny chick') were related to the feminine stereotypes that are particularly common in slang, usually used in negative ways to describe a woman wearing too much make-up. Nonetheless, it has not distorted the general depiction of the brand through the eyes of the participants, as one may decode patterns exhibiting a girls' brand set in a couture world of fashion creations and fearless imaginations.

Nostalgic perception of LEGO brand

Generation X participants were presented with three images representing LEGO building sets, each representing seemingly different variants of the product. These included:

A LEGO Galaxy Explorer *(a nostalgic new one referring to the past)*
B LEGO City Wildlife Rescue Operation *(a current one)*
C LEGO Castle Black Falcon's Fortress *(a nostalgic old one from the past).*

One of the first things that strike one is that among all toy brands, LEGO, regardless of the age of those involved, appeared to be a brand that has caused much discussion already at the stage of displaying image stimuli. Moreover, the presented images automatically engendered a desire to own each of the depicted sets. Specifically, the way the participants acted implicitly suggested purchasing toys for themselves. Some interviewees admitted to owning one by saying out loud, '*I have this set*' or '*Hey, I remember I have had that set*'. This further confirms that the image stimuli were well suited to the subjects of the study.

There was a tendency among Xers to go for the third option, which was the nostalgic old variant of the LEGO model. The interest in buying the nostalgic new set was already two times lower, albeit there seemed to be a shared understanding of the LEGO themes the kits were representing (specifically *LEGO Space*, that dates back to 1978, as being depicted in the 2022's Galaxy Explorer model being a remake of the 1979 *Classic Space's* Galaxy Explorer). It must be acknowledged, though, that not a single person in Generation X would take possession of the latest LEGO model. It must be noted here that LEGO was difficult to reach for Xers, unlike for generations Y and Z, because of the political and economic environment straining on the leash of the Soviet Union's impact.

Generation Y participants were presented with three images representing LEGO building sets, each representing seemingly different variants of the product. These included

A LEGO Pirates of Barracuda Bay *(a nostalgic new one referring to the past)*
B LEGO City Wildlife Rescue Operation *(a current one)*
C LEGO Knights' Kingdom King Leo's Castle *(a nostalgic old one from the past).*

There was a tie between the new nostalgic variant (a reference to the 1989's pirate ship Black Seas Barracuda) and the old nostalgic LEGO model (the castle from the *Castle Knights' Kingdom* theme). Interestingly, Generation X preferred the old nostalgic variant while Ys leaned towards the new nostalgic one. Participants' comments reflected the want to acquire all three displayed models, which is quite a common practice among LEGO consumers. Indeed, some men do not purchase LEGO due to the bricks' functional capabilities; instead, they make fine additions to their private collections. One male participant stated, '*I already have the second one, so . . . [smile]*'. And so that must be why three men in Generation Y might have decided to purchase the current kit. The authors therefore reasoned that some choices could be altered unless a person had the specific model lying on the shelf at home.

Generation Z participants were presented with three images representing LEGO building sets, each representing seemingly different variants of the product. These included the following:

A LEGO City Wildlife Rescue Operation (*a current one*)
B LEGO Creator 3in1 Viking Ship and the Midgard Serpent *(a nostalgic new one referring to the past)*
C LEGO City Airport *(a nostalgic old one from the past)*

Following the focus group interview with the Millennials, the authors emphasised to the participants in Generation Z that they are to choose only one LEGO set. Participants answered with faint, quizzical smiles. The observations indicated that Zs performed significantly better in terms of propensity towards the new nostalgic model, which contrasts with Xers' preferences, who, as written earlier, were inclined to older kits, no longer accessible, but still sitting in their memory. The distribution of responses for the current *LEGO City*-themed set and the old nostalgic version of Airport was one and the same. Although Zs did not comment on whether or not they owned any of the portrayed LEGO kits, it cannot be excluded that the way they responded would reflect the actual state of possessing the LEGO set. That is, if they appeared to own the pictured set, they would be constrained to choose from the remaining two options. Another explanation would be that the stimuli were so captivating that it was challenging for them to pick just one.

The authors asked the participants the following question: '*What is the first word that comes to your mind when seeing the displayed logo?*'. No sooner had the illustrious brick-shaped logo with a vibrant red colour appeared on the screen than the participants cranked out tonnes of words connoted to the renowned Danish toy manufacturer. In this vein, LEGO was the most conspicuous brand among the six toy brands chosen for the study and, concurrently, the one that has yielded the most homogeneous collection of personal reminiscences. Specifically, most of these recollections conveyed a narrative of a brick set – an object of an insatiable desire that has been longed for by someone who, as a child, had been conjuring up pictures of himself indulging in imaginative play of building creative constructions. Seldom would some of these dreams materialise owing to the already staggering price tag since the vast majority of parents had not been capable of purchasing the coveted sets.

Having experienced the disappointment of unsatisfied longings, with their wings clipped, even after all these years of dream frustrations, they would eventually attain the unattainable through the purchase of a set, of which the design resembled the original one. As one male Millennial revealed,

> *I remember a small antiquarian bookshop near my neighbourhood. They had been selling outlet LEGO sets from the late 1990s. Among them was the one my heart greatly desired, a Duel on Tatooine [7101] from 'The Phantom Menace' subtheme. It included minifigures of Qui-Gon Jinn and Darth Maul on a speeder bike. The latter had long been considered a rare figurine since he got featured in two sets in 1999. It was devastating for me to discover that the set had sold out. Never had I felt so dejected, as if a part of me had just died. Only after many years of longing would I follow my innate inclination to possessiveness and eventually acquire this set [the 2015 redesigned set 75096].*

This quote illustrates the paradoxical essence of nostalgia, which is the theme of loss. Loss of possession, according to Belk,[34] is an element of the sacralisation ethos revolving around collecting valued material possessions. The craving imbued into this LEGO set, as reflected by the participant, appears to be so passionate that the fire of desire that emerged from an interplay of imagination is even greater. Hence, desired objects are often worshipped and canonised, as evident in this toy brand.

In stark contrast to this bitter portrayal of nostalgia was another reminiscence evoked by a female post-Millennial.

> *When I was twelve, I had to have my gallbladder removed. I was scared of the surgery as I had to be under anaesthesia. My mum consoled me that it feels like taking a nap and promised me that once I wake up, there will be a surprise waiting for me. The surgeons said the operation had succeeded. Barely had I opened my eyes when I saw a LEGO*

Figure 4.4 Word cloud reflecting the participant's perception of 'LEGO'

> *Harry Potter box set standing next to my hospital bed – the one I had always wanted to have, Hogwarts Express [75955]. I had forgotten about post-surgical pain.*

A few more narratives were being told in this vein, whereby an exquisite LEGO set was to reward children's courage to undergo surgery.

Still on the subject of the Danish brand is an unusually accurate reflection made by the older member of Gen X embracing the idea of a 'smart toy'.

> *I believe that the world is heading towards the absolute stupidity, specifically in companies' orientation towards consumers. LEGO, in resistance to its competitors, has been and still is the incarnation of an educational toy. So long as they stick to this premise, then my choice will always be the LEGO bricks, for I want my grandchildren to be cleverer.*

Whether considered an 'educational toy' or an object of childhood's fierce desire, the word cloud indicates that LEGO withstood decades by adapting and pushing to the limits of the simple brick, consistently capturing kids' imaginations across generations.

Nostalgic perception of Transformers brand

Generation X participants were presented with three images representing Hasbro's Transformers-themed toy line, each representing seemingly different variants of the product:

A Studio Series 87 Deluxe Class BUMBLEBEE ('Dark of the Moon') *(a current one)*;

B Generations Legacy Deluxe DEAD END Action Figure *(a nostalgic new one referring to the past)*;
C G1 Autobot Commander OPTIMUS PRIME *(a nostalgic old one from the past)*.

Among the available options, the 2022 edition of Bumblebee emerged as the dominant preference for buying a Transformers toy, which seemed to be influenced by the participants' awareness of the Michael Bay film, or it was in the character that linked it with the franchise. A male participant immediately stated Bumblebee, '*the yellow one*', was '*distinguishable from other toys in the cluster*'. The authors believe this was a prevalent view among several other participants in Generation X. The younger Xers, born somewhere between 1975 and 1980, apparently recognised the names of Optimus and Bumblebee. One female participant, the same who had frowned disapprovingly upon the Power Rangers-themed toy line, called Transformers '*space freaks*'. The eldest participant, in the same vein, enquired whether the depicted toys were truly suited for them.

Generation Y participants were presented with three images representing Hasbro's Transformers-themed toy line, each representing seemingly different variants of the product:

A Cybertron: Robots in Disguise STARSCREAM (Supreme Class) *(a nostalgic old one from the past)*;
B Studio Series 87 Deluxe Class BUMBLEBEE ('Dark of the Moon') *(a nostalgic new one referring to the past)*;
C Generations G2 Legacy Voyager LASER OPTIMUS PRIME *(a current one)*.

The 2022 edition of Bumblebee, which served to exemplify a contemporary variant of the toy during the interview with Generation X, acted as a nostalgic stimulus for the Millennials. Regardless of the changes, the renowned yellow Autobot was still the most sought-after toy. Many participants invoked the 2007 film in the discussion that followed, thereby signifying why Bumblebee has prevailed over other options. It may be said that Millennials have a genuine liking for that character. The second most popular choice was the *Cybertron*-themed version of Starscream, one of the main villains in the Transformers universe. Specifically, it is believed that given their massive weaponry, toys instantiating villains would seem more enticing to buy. Intriguingly, the action figure of Optimus Prime, the movie's supposed hero, was once again the least popular option, as it had occurred in Generation X.

Generation Z participants were presented with three images representing Hasbro's Transformers-themed toy line, each representing seemingly different variants of the product:

A Transformers Movie Deluxe BUMBLEBEE ('08 Camaro) *(a nostalgic old one from the past)*;

B Studio Series 84 Deluxe Class IRONHIDE ('Bumblebee') *(a nostalgic new one referring to the past)*;
C Cyber Commander series OPTIMUS PRIME *(a current one)*.

For the third straight time, Bumblebee was the leading choice in Generation Z, and for the third time, Optimus failed to impress. Absurdly odd, as it appears, the franchise's alleged protagonist has been found to be less popular than he was meant to be. In addition, no matter which variant of the toy the image epitomised, the yellow robot certainly won the hearts of the study's participants. On the plus side, the participants were predisposed to lean towards the ancillary characters like Starscream or Ironhide, knowing fully well that they were free to choose the better-known character. Yet it cannot be ruled out that such robots were deemed awesome enough in the eyes of the participants once they saw their portrayal in the cluster. Though it was possible to identify the nostalgia-induced behaviour peculiarly among male representatives of generations Y and Z, it is just conceivable that Xers would follow the pattern.

The authors asked the participants the following question: '*What is the first word that comes to your mind when seeing the displayed logo?*'. Transformers, regretfully, is another exemplar of a brand bearing the hallmarks of tumult sparked by the imposition of communism in Poland, as the image of the brand evoked by the participants was at odds with the creator's purport encapsulated in the toyline. Although the word 'Transformer' suggests a toy that can transform from a vehicle to a robot character and vice versa, participants' associations resulted from watching a pentalogy of films directed by Michael Bay. The majority of participants in generations Y and Z had clear connections to the actress Megan Fox as if being synonymous with the movies, though she had appeared on screen only twice. Indeed, the most recurring words used by participants in the Millennial and post-Millennial generations exhibited an image of the film depicting 'explosions', 'Bumblebee', the film's apparent protagonist, and slow-motion shots of 'Megan Fox' – all that accompanied by an end-credits song by 'Linkin Park'. In the first place, as it has occurred, participants would be more reflective on the film, followed by the cartoon and ending with the toy. Technically, it should be the other way around, given that 'Transformers' is one of the few exceptions whose success has been founded not on media adaptations, but on a toy line.

Precisely because of the aforementioned yoke of communism, most of the Western brand goods, including the merchandise of international toy companies, had been either inaccessible or acquirable in exchange for foreign currency, preferably the US dollar, at Pewex hard-currency shops. Never has there been a devotedness to the brand in Polish boys as had happened in America or Japan much earlier. Conversely, child's play in Poland long had been oriented towards collective experiences within group

Figure 4.5 Word cloud reflecting the participant's perception of 'Transformers'

members of the same generation. Somewhat paradoxically, it is the small things, be it a ball, a jumping rope, or everyday deeds of ordinary folk, that engender collective identity among people. As a 57-year-old male Gen Xer asserted,

> *My generation [1965–1975] had derived more enjoyment out of communal life together rather than ascribing utmost values to just a toy. Naturally, that [a toy] also offered a temporary escape from the grey reality, but it was in the carefree hours spent in the vicinity of the neighbourhood that we socialised with each other.*

Therefore, not a soul in focus groups could associate the brand with 'Japan' or with a 'tin can' – the words that connote the origins of the Transformers, of which mechanical tin toys known as *Henshin*, made of recycled food cans, have transformed into a worldwide phenomenon. Nevertheless, 'innovation' was at least the mere characteristic conveying the Japanese component of the image that materialised in the word cloud.

Nostalgic perception of Pokémon brand

Generation X participants were presented with three images representing the Pokémon-themed toy line, each representing seemingly different variants of the product:

A SANDSLASH Pokémon Monster Collection Tomy Figure *(a nostalgic old one from the past)*;

B Pokémon Select Articulated Figure – CHARIZARD *(a nostalgic new one referring to the past)*;
C Pokémon PIKACHU Plush Stuffed Animal – Winking – Large 12" *(a current one)*.

In startling contrast to what the authors have learnt during interviews with subjects in Generation X about Power Rangers and Transformers, as regards the cognisance of the brand, Pokémon seemed far more recognisable than the latter two combined. Already the authors would hear the name Pikachu once the image cluster featuring the franchise's flagship mascot was displayed. That being said, the plush stuffed animal toy of Pikachu, released as part of the 2022 merchandise, was the absolute winner and hence was no longer depicted so as to avoid bias in generations Y and Z. Charizard, the nostalgic variant of a toy, released to celebrate the 25th anniversary of the Game Boy video game, was the second most favourable choice, losing by a margin of a single vote. Not surprisingly, only one person, the youngest of males in Generation X, would pick Sandslash, emblematic of the 'Monster Collection' line of collectible Pokémon figures that have been sold since the late 1990s.

Generation Y participants were presented with three images representing the Pokémon-themed toy line, each representing seemingly different variants of the product:

A HISUIAN GROWLITHE Poké Plush ('Pokémon Legends: Arceus') *(a current one)*;
B Hasbro's CHARMANDER with Electronic Voice and Light-Up Tail *(a nostalgic old one from the past)*;
C Pokémon Throw 'N' Pop Duel PIKACHU, Pokeball & CUBONE, Repeat Ball *(a nostalgic new one referring to the past)*.

The focal images of toys that were displayed therein required Millennials to exhibit some degree of acquaintance with the franchise, and judging from their behavioural expression of attention to the stimuli, they indeed were. Specifically, the subjects seemed to be running towards nostalgia as they opted for the battle pack evoking the iconic Takara Tomy's 'Master Ball' sets (distributed in the US market under the name of 'Grabber Ball'), where one could compete with other players in one-on-one battle between their Pokémon, just as portrayed in the anime. Battle packs were arguably the best-selling toy products at the height of the boom in 2000 as an inevitable consequence of the much-awaited premiere on Polish television.

Among the most notable observations was that participants complained about omitting the legendary *Pokémon Trading Card Game* in the image set. While the authors initially intended to feature the graphical representation of the collectible cards, such an overinterpretation would have distorted what is labelled as a toy.

The second most coveted toy was the interactive electronic figurine of Charmander from 1998. Along with Squirtle and Bulbasaur, Charmander was one of the three Pokémon destined to be one's 'First Partner' in the beginning of the Nintendo game, so it was expectable that the toy would place this high. Since the Millennials' attention spread over the nostalgic and old variants of the toys, recalling enduring memories of childhood, almost none have thought about the Hisuian Growlithe stuffed animal toy. Just one girl in her twenties favoured the Poké Plush toy amid its presumed fluffy texture.

Generation Z participants were presented with three images representing the Pokémon-themed toy line, each representing seemingly different variants of the product:

A Pokémon Articulated Battle Figure LUCARIO *(a nostalgic new one referring to the past)*;
B Pokémon Diamond & Pearl Deluxe Electronic Series 1 DIALGA Action Figure *(a nostalgic old one from the past)*;
C HISUIAN GROWLITHE Poké Plush ('Pokémon Legends: Arceus') *(a current one)*.

The remarkable journey of the Pokémon franchise has prevailed for the next 25 anime seasons and over 122 video games, thus expanding its universe with more bizarre species. Therefore, the authors have decided to include *Diamond and Pearl* characters, tailored for post-Millennials, so as to indicate that resultant behaviour to stimuli had nothing to do with the figures' high-profile status. It is striking to note that participants in Generation Z, just as occurred earlier with LEGO, were homogenously favouring the likes of an old nostalgic toy model over the nostalgic new one and present variants of the toy, respectively. Conversely, Millennials did it the other way round – they mostly preferred the new nostalgic variant, followed by the nostalgic old-fangled and the current one. And so, the 2007 edition of the Dialga action figure claimed the top spot as Z's most favourite toy, with the Lucario figurine and the Growlithe Poké plush reaching a stalemate. Notably, the same stuffed animal toy epitomising Growlithe, a mascot being part of the merchandise announcing the latest video game *Pokémon Legends: Arceus*, was repeatedly displayed to Generation Z participants as well to determine whether or not their bond with the brand has endured. The findings indicated that the bond is being nurtured, as the subjects seemed to have been in the loop with the most recent episodes of the anime. Incidentally, some of them owned a Nintendo Switch console – the only device that appears to support the latest Pokémon games. Back in the day, Millennials had to buy Game Boy, Game Boy Color, or Game Boy Advance to experience the coveted and beloved Pokémon world. As they grew older, their knowledge of the franchise may have been limited to times when they were younger, hence the Millennials' preference towards more cognisant Pokémon species.

The authors asked the participants the following question: '*What is the first word that comes to your mind when seeing the displayed logo?*'. Without mentioning the name of 'Pikachu', an instantly recognisable mascot of the franchise, howbeit no longer the most popular one, according to the latest study,[35] it appears to be rather a vain endeavour to converse about Pokémon. When people think of the brand, it is usually the iconic yellow mouse that first comes to mind. Perhaps it is in this chubby rodent-like creature that conveys easily recognisable references to the Japanese anime series, allowing people in Generation X to grasp the rudimentary principles of the franchise's premise. Commenting on this background, a female participant in Generation X revealed, '*I am overly familiar with the anime, albeit it ain't the same cognitive framework. It is just not my generation, you [the authors] see*'.

The main motives that were mentioned in the Millennials focus group were associated with individuals' private experiences dating back to the origins of the Polish Pokémon fad, reaching its height in the years between 2000 and 2001. Undoubtedly, one of the hallmarks incorporated into this phenomenon was Tazos – small round discs that could be found in bags of potato chips made by Lay's. Indeed, 'Tazos', 'chips', and 'Lay's' were the most recurring words that emerged during the interviews and hence had the most emphasis on the Millennials' perception of the brand. Some would often recall hand-groping chip bags before the purchase to make sure that the coveted Tazo was inside. Although Frito-Lay released Tazos to mimic Pogs, a children's game originally played with milk caps, its commercial success was due to its collectible values. However, what stirred tremendous covetousness among Millennials and Gen Zs were cards from the trading game, with new sets of cards constantly penetrating the market, collecting the hearts of the next generations. The re-release of the video game adaptation, enthrallingly, was introduced in 2014 on the Nintendo 3DS console. This perfectly illustrates the evolution from the physical socialisation of Millennial aficionados to the intangible augmented reality of post-Millennials; be that as it may, losing the art of playing outdoors.

With that being said, many males lamented the lack of Pokémon TCG cards as an option to choose from in the first part of the study. In relation to cards, one participant recalled,

> *I remember a schoolmate who had been collecting these [cards], keeping them in a ring binder. For whole days I had been longing for an English course we had been both enrolled in, whereby I would browse through his splendid collection of Pokémon. On the day when he graduated from primary school, he gave me a golden card of Entei [a legendary Pokémon] as a token of our short friendship.*

Figure 4.6 Word cloud reflecting the participant's perception of 'Pokémon'

Altogether, the word cloud has the most emphasis on the 'lifestyle', one that involves assembling a collection of Pokémon creatures and hence sharing commonalities with mates, while others see it, be that as it may, as 'scurrying around the streets' with a cyber-world being displayed on the smartphone screen.

Nostalgic perception of my little pony brand

Generation X participants were presented with three images representing Hasbro's My Little Pony-themed toy line, each representing seemingly different variants of the product:

- A My Little Pony 35th Anniversary MOONSTONE Rainbow Collection Pony *(a nostalgic new one referring to the past)*;
- B My Little Pony: Sparkling Generations SUNNY STARSCOUT G5 Pony *(a current one)*;
- C My Little Pony G1 Earth Pony LICKETY SPLIT *(a nostalgic old one from the past)*.

Continuing the pattern established in Power Rangers hereinabove, Xers' seemed evenly divided between the new nostalgic one and the present variant, forsaking the likes of the original pony from 1982 in favour of the former two products. Minimally, the figurine Sunny Starscout, incarnating the fifth generation of the My Little Pony toyline, was picked more often. Conversely to what has been observed in Barbie, enthrallingly, males would usually buy the nostalgic pony, whereas women preferred the modern-day toy as it was perceived to be in vogue. Quite boldly, Hasbro seems to have been directing their efforts to preserve the glimpse of fantasy the creators had wanted to convey in G1 ponies, thereby targeting Xers with resultant rereleases. Because females leaned towards the 2022 toy, the authors found it quite questionable whether or not pursuing such a one-sided strategy would succeed in the Polish market, unbeknownst to the brand. It was noticeable that Xers evinced no deeper relationship with the brand. Commenting on this background, a female participant flatly declared, '*In no way have I felt the connection to the toy*'.

Generation Y participants were presented with three images representing Hasbro's My Little Pony-themed toy line, each representing seemingly different variants of the product:

A My Little Pony: Sparkling Generations SUNNY STARSCOUT G5 Pony *(a current one)*;
B My Little Pony PINKIE PIE Glitter Celebration Wave 2 G3 Pony *(a nostalgic old one from the past)*;
C My Little Pony RAINBOW DASH Retro G3 Pony *(a nostalgic new one referring to the past).*

One could immediately sense the participants' aversion towards the brand, given the preliminary reluctance to choose any of the displayed toys. It certainly reflected a hedonic motivation, yet an alternative one, of which behaviour directs an individual away from engaging in an activity regarded through its 'inherent unpleasantness', as Lewin[36] would say. The new nostalgic variant took the lead, followed by the present and the old nostalgic variant. Of particular note is the toy company's seemingly different approach towards the Millennials, releasing the 'fourth generation' of toys, which characters actually resemble the 'third generation' with an evolved design. Not only is such a solution adjusted to target new consumers (Generation Z in this regard), but more probably, the board of Hasbro seems to have made a real-life experiment to see if Millennials are inclined to nostalgia to the same extent as Xers are. Again, these were males that were predisposed to buy the new nostalgic toy. Paralleling the behavioural patterns observed among men in Generation X, they felt disposed to the figurine of a pony with a light blue coat and a rainbowish mane. One female Millennial confessed to having owned the G3 pony, just the same as the one being displayed; regrettably, this has not been followed by an intimate narrative thereafter.

Generation Z participants were presented with three images representing Hasbro's My Little Pony-themed toy line, each representing seemingly different variants of the product:

A My Little Pony: See Your Sparkle IZZY MOONBOW G5 Pony *(a current one)*;
B My Little Pony SDCC 2019 TWILIGHT SPARKLE Brushable Pony *(a nostalgic new one referring to the past)*;
C My Little Pony RAINBOW DASH Special Release G3.5 Pony *(a nostalgic old one from the past).*

In stark contrast to what has occurred during previous focus group meetings, the participants unanimously did not even consider the present variant. Most of the responses expressed disgust, discomfort, and unpleasantness. For example, a male participant asserted that '*the pony on the left*' seemed repulsive to him with its bluish mane and '*preposterous design*'. Females, in turn, reckoned it '*a badly made toy*'. In this case, the authors conjecture that the fifth generation of the 'My Little Pony' toyline, which started in 2021, aims at the alpha generation (2011+), hence a chilly reception from the Zs. Furthermore, what catches the eye is the altered design of ponies' muzzles, disturbingly bearing a close resemblance to human faces. Under those circumstances, almost everyone in Generation Z picked the new nostalgic variant of the toy. Another female participant hinted at why they would choose to buy a nostalgic toy. Twilight Sparkle is an Alicorn – a pony having both a unicorn horn and Pegasus wings. This, in turn, implies a kind of utilitarian motivation where the more articulation a pony figurine has, the more play the children will have. A few individuals, men to be specific, favoured the old nostalgic variant of the toy. Astonishingly, it was an instantiation of a blue pony with rainbowish details emblazoned on it – arguably the same set of identifiers that mustered men's general fondness for this type of pony.

The authors asked the participants the following question: '*What is the first word that comes to your mind when seeing the displayed logo?*'. In some ways, the brand raised more questions than it answered. There was a tendency for participants in generations Y and Z to operate with primary reference to 'ponies', thus reflecting a shared understanding of the brand's core product – equines intended for fantasy-loving little girls. Nonetheless, this association was not so straightforward for Xers, of whom some have urged the authors to elucidate what type of toys the brand sells, oblivious to the fact that they just saw the ponies a few minutes ago. Moreover, there was no discernible indication that Xers would be acquainted with the 'My Little Pony' franchise. However, a Gen X woman said her first thought was of the cartoon, though she has never been involved with the toy brand by any means. 'Cartoon' was the second most prominent word highlighted in the word cloud, which reflected the participants' familiarity with the animated show, appearing to be more attributed to the children's TV series than the merchandise itself.

Although the vast majority of associations provided by the participants suggest a favourable, unspoiled image of the brand, it is paradoxical that Millennials and post-Millennials have exhibited mixed to unfavourable reactions

Figure 4.7 Word cloud reflecting the participant's perception of 'My Little Pony'

that had been hinted at in the first part of the study. Moreover, their reluctance seemed so insurmountable that the authors had to go to extreme lengths to make them put forward any association. Post-Millennials were more inclined to express abhorrence towards the brand, particularly its latest releases, with Millennials preferring not to speak. This rather aberrative display did not affect the word cloud, for 'strange' was the only common comment among Ys and Zs that materialised. After all, most of the girls, especially in Generation Z, could tell the authors the names of 'Twilight Sparkle' and 'Fluttershy', thereby revealing their accustomedness to the '*Friendship is Magic*' series. It is important to note that among the most frequent associations decoding the participant's image of the 'My Little Pony' brand, 'fantasy', and 'magic', the founding values that defined the franchise were snubbed. Instead, many participants would recall 'Kuce z Bronxu' (translated in English as 'Ponies from Bronx'), an Internet parody in a format of brief sketches depicting a grotesque representation of the original show's characters, looking like they were made in MS Paint.

4.4 Summary of the findings

The findings of qualitative research enable the formulation of conclusions of a cognitive and application nature. In this way, focus groups elicit qualitative information, which is analysed to understand hitherto neglected phenomena. Used in a supplementary fashion, the six focus groups served as an antecedent step to quantitative analyses in the second stage of the research procedure. In almost all cases, the choice experiment confirmed that previous experience with the brand, especially during childhood, influenced the consumers' response to nostalgic toys. When they knew the brand, the participants always opted to purchase a toy referring to the times of their youth. When the brand was less known, or its profile was incongruent with the target audience (e.g., boys and 'Barbie', and girls and 'Transformers'), the participants seemed to be predisposed to choose the present variant of the toy as the safe pick. This applied in particular to individuals in Generation X, whose lack of cognisance of some focal brands has affected their preferences. Although they seemed evenly divided between the nostalgic and the most current versions, it was the contemporary toy that was picked more often. Specifically, the people in Generation X have posed constraints, for this unfamiliarity epitomised another problem that is not identifiable in Western countries, namely, the impact of communism in Poland. It should be noted that post-Millennials displayed differences in expressing nostalgia as contrasted to generations X and Y. Contrariwise, in some cases, participants in Generation Z were inclined to go for the plain old toy, thereby expressing the desire to retreat to times of their childhood. Or in other words, to reclaim the possession of an object that promises an escape from the unsatisfactory present.[37] While a new nostalgic toy, as favoured by Millennials, with its resemblances to the classic plaything, serves as a totem of the past times, the propensity to take the older toy implies a desire to relive the joys of their childhood once again.

The in-depth tradition of probing for profound information, derived from ethnographic practices, is essential for uncovering deeper processes in individuals, hence providing insights into behaviour.[38] The data for this study are derived from asking the participants to conjure associations with pictorial representations of the focal brand logos. As the subjects started to present their ideas, a discussion was initiated, focusing on the shared experience with every six brands. The content of these self-disclosures indicated instances of nostalgic behaviour in participants as manifested in densely structured memoirs, connected by a theme of 'childhood'. The most discernible type of nostalgia in participants was 'personal nostalgia', of which narratives conveyed the sentimentality towards a specific person, usually a family member – a giver, thus underscoring a strong relation. Echoing Csikszentmihalyi and Rochberg-Halton,[39] toys are momentous objects shaping the self in early childhood. Moreover, being given as presents, toys act as a medium between the child and the bestower. They help an individual cherish the memory of loved ones, and when they pass away, such a toy becomes a convenient means of storing the memories depicting one's own past.[40] As a result, many of these reminiscences would usually evoke a portrayal of a family member whose gifts were regarded as evidence of love from a significant human being, as Belk[41] would have put it. Some disclosures evinced that owning a popular toy was an antecedent step to claiming affiliation with a group of like-minded individuals as a part of a micro-ritual entailing the shared use (play) of the product. Through these memberships, they would define their social identity in congruence with the perceived external image of a social group. Play, the extraction of utility from the toy product, exists through intergroup relations between individuals coalesced by a common passion.

Hence, the participants must have gone to extraordinary lengths to maintain a positive social identity by retaining membership within the attractive collective entity. Embracing Alexander's[42] understanding of culture as a textual manifestation, nostalgia is a dynamic social text whose motifs are 'a carefree childhood', 'a family member', 'dreams', 'a promise', 'collection', and 'belongingness'.

The findings from the qualitative study have allowed the authors to widen the scope of the previous analyses regarding the attitudes and behaviour of Polish consumers towards nostalgic brands of toys as a result of establishing the groups' cohesiveness in each focus group where in-depth accounts could be shared in a spontaneous, unconstrained manner. The data collected from culturally relevant members representing Polish consumers were particularly persuasive.

Notes

1 Gołąb-Andrzejak, "Konsumenci Pokolenia Y – Nowe Wyzwanie dla Komunikacji Marketingowej", 141.
2 Bloor et al., *Focus Groups in Social Research*, 8.
3 Goldman, "The Group Depth Interview", 62.
4 Morgan, *Focus Groups as Qualitative Research*, 2.
5 Catterall and Maclaran, "Focus Group Data and Qualitative Analysis Programs: Coding the Moving Picture as Well as the Snapshots", 42.
6 Kitzinger, "The Methodology of Focus Groups: The Importance of Interaction Between Research Participants", 107.
7 Doody et al., "Focus Group Interviews in Nursing Research: Part 1", 6.
8 Jourard, *The Transparent Self*, 9.
9 Willig, *Introducing Qualitative Research in Psychology*, 31.
10 Jourard, *The Transparent Self*, 10.
11 Krueger and Casey, *Focus Groups: A Practical Guide for Applied Research*, 30.
12 Goldman, "The Group Depth Interview", 61–62.
13 Goldman, "The Group Depth Interview", 61–62.
14 Krueger and Casey, *Focus Groups: A Practical Guide for Applied Research*, 30.
15 Morgan, "Focus Groups".
16 Doody et al., "Focus Group Interviews in Nursing Research: Part 1", 18.
17 Merriam and Tisdell, *Qualitative Research: A Guide to Design and Implementation*, 16.
18 Morgan, *Focus Groups as Qualitative Research*, 13.
19 Lee, *Using Qualitative Methods in Organizational Research*, 72.
20 Merton and Kendall, "The Focussed Interview", 541.
21 Stewart et al., *Focus Groups: Theory and Practice*, 17.
22 Sierra and McQuitty, "Attitudes and Emotions as Determinants of Nostalgia Purchases: An Application of Social Identity Theory", 109.
23 Stewart et al., *Focus Groups: Theory and Practice*, 10.
24 Goldman, "The Group Depth Interview", 62.

25 Bray et al., "An Exploratory Study into the Factors Impeding Ethical Consumption", 601.
26 Stiles, "Pictorial Representation", 127.
27 Tighe, "Worldwide Revenue of Major Toy Companies in 2021 (in Million U.S. Dollars)".
28 Belk, "Attachment to Possessions", 40.
29 Belk, "Possessions and the Sense of Past", 115.
30 Authors note: In 2022, LEGO announced its first-time ever collaboration with Hasbro to bring fully converting LEGO Optimus Prime set. It is unknown whether or not the Transformers project will be continued.
31 Muehling et al., "Exploring the Boundaries of Nostalgic Advertising Effects: A Consideration of Childhood Brand Exposure and Attachment on Consumers' Responses to Nostalgia-Themed Advertisements", 76.
32 Brown, "Let's Do the Time Warp Again: A Marketing Manifesto for Retro Revolutionaries", 125–139.
33 Brown et al., "Teaching Old Brands New Tricks: Retro Branding and the Revival of Brand Meaning", 21.
34 Belk, "Possessions and the Extended Self", 142–143.
35 Miller, "Research Claims to Reveal the 10 Most Popular Pokémon, and Pikachu Isn't One of Them".
36 Lewin, *The Conceptual Representation and the Measurement of Psychological Forces*, 25–29.
37 Belk et al., "The Fire of Desire: A Multi-Sited Inquiry Into Consumer Passion", 335.
38 Krueger and Casey, *Focus Groups: A Practical Guide for Applied Research*, 43.
39 Csikszentmihalyi and Halton, *The Meaning of Things: Domestic Symbols and the Self*, 92.
40 Belk, "Attachment to Possessions", 40.
41 Belk, "Possessions and the Extended Self", 149.
42 Alexander, *The Meaning of Social Life: A Cultural Sociology*, 13.

Reference list

Alexander, Jeffrey C. *The Meaning of Social Life: A Cultural Sociology*. New York: Oxford University Press, 2003. https://doi.org/10.1093/acprof:oso/9780195160840.001.0001.

Belk, Russell W. "Attachment to Possessions." In *Place Attachment*, 37–62. Boston: Springer, 1992. https://doi.org/10.1007/978-1-4684-8753-4_3.

Belk, Russell W. "Possessions and the Extended Self." *Journal of Consumer Research* 15, no. 2 (1988): 139–168. https://doi.org/10.1086/209154.

Belk, Russell W. "Possessions and the Sense of Past." *Odyssey* (1991): 114–130.

Belk, Russell W., Güliz Ger, and Askegaard, Søren. "The Fire of Desire: A Multi-Sited Inquiry Into Consumer Passion." *Journal of Consumer Research* 30, no. 3 (2003): 326–351. https://doi.org/10.1086/378613.

Bloor, Michael, Jane Frankland, Michelle Thomas, and Kate Robson. *Focus Groups in Social Research*. Thousand Oaks, CA: SAGE, 2001. https://doi.org/10.4135/9781849209175.

Bray, Jeffrey, Nick Johns, and David Kilburn. "An Exploratory Study into the Factors Impeding Ethical Consumption." *Journal of Business Ethics* 98, no. 4 (2011): 597–608. https://doi.org/10.1007/s10551-010-0640-9.

Brown, Steven. "Let's Do the Time Warp Again: A Marketing Manifesto for Retro Revolutionaries." In *The Future of Marketing*, edited by P. J. Kitchen, 125–139. Basingstoke: Palgrave Macmillan, 2003.

Brown, Steven, R. V. Kozinets, and Jonh Sherry. "Teaching Old Brands New Tricks: Retro Branding and the Revival of Brand Meaning." *Journal of Marketing* 67, no. 1 (2003): 19–33. https://doi.org/10.1509/jmkg.67.3.19.18657.

Catterall, M., and Pauline Maclaran. "Focus Group Data and Qualitative Analysis Programs: Coding the Moving Picture as Well as the Snapshots." *Sociological Research Online* 2, no. 1 (1997): 41–49.

Csikszentmihalyi, Mihaly, and Eugene Halton. *The Meaning of Things: Domestic Symbols and the Self*. Cambridge: Cambridge University Press, 1981. https://doi.org/10.2307/2067526.

Doody, Owen, Eamonn Slevin, and Laurens Taggart. "Focus Group Interviews in Nursing Research: Part 1." *British Journal of Nursing* 22, no. 1 (2013): 16–19. https://doi.org/10.12968/bjon.2013.22.1.16.

Gołąb-Andrzejak, Edyta. "Konsumenci Pokolenia Y – Nowe Wyzwanie dla Komunikacji Marketingowej." *Handel Wewnętrzny* 2, no. 361 (2016): 140–151.

Goldman, Alfred. "The Group Depth Interview." *Journal of Marketing* 26, no. 3 (1962): 61–68. https://doi.org/10.1177/0022242962026003.

Jourard, Sidney M. *The Transparent Self*. New York: Van Nostrand Reinhold, 1964.

Kitzinger, Jenny. "The Methodology of Focus Groups: The Importance of Interaction Between Research Participants." *Sociology of Health and Illness* 16, no. 1 (1994): 103–121.

Krueger, Richard A., and Mary Anne Casey. *Focus Groups: A Practical Guide for Applied Research*. 5th ed. Thousand Oaks, CA: SAGE, 2015.

Lee, Thomas W. *Using Qualitative Methods in Organizational Research*. Thousand Oaks, CA: SAGE, 1999.

Lewin, Kurt. *The Conceptual Representation and the Measurement of Psychological Forces*. Durham, NC: Duke University Press, 1938. https://doi.org/10.1037/13613-000.

Merriam, Sharah B., and Elizabeth J. Tisdell. *Qualitative Research: A Guide to Design and Implementation*. 4th ed. San Francisco, CA: Jossey-Bass, 2016.

Merton, Robert K., and Patricia L. Kendall. "The Focussed Interview." *American Journal of Sociology* 51, no. 1 (1946): 541–557.

Miller, Christine. "Research Claims to Reveal the 10 Most Popular Pokémon, and Pikachu Isn't One of Them." *GameRant*, December 19, 2022. Accessed February 9, 2023. https://gamerant.com/study-10-most-popular-pokemon-no-pikachu/.

Morgan, David. "Focus Groups." In *Approaches to Qualitative Research: A Reader on Theory and Practice*, edited by S. Hesse-Biber and P. Leavy, 266–268. New York: Oxford University Press, 2004.

Morgan, David. *Focus Groups as Qualitative Research*. Thousand Oaks, CA: SAGE, 1997.

Muehling, Daniel D., David E. Sprott, and Abdullah Sultan. "Exploring the Boundaries of Nostalgic Advertising Effects: A Consideration of Childhood Brand Exposure and Attachment on Consumers' Responses to Nostalgia-Themed Advertisements." *Journal of Advertising* 43, no. 1 (2014): 73–84. https://doi.org/10.1080/00913367.2013.815110.

Sierra, Jeremy J., and Shaun McQuitty. "Attitudes and Emotions as Determinants of Nostalgia Purchases: An Application of Social Identity Theory." *Journal of Marketing Theory and Practice* 15, no. 2 (2007): 99–112.

Stewart, David W., P. N. Shamdasani, and D. W. Rook. *Focus Groups: Theory and Practice*. 2nd ed. London: SAGE, 2007. https://doi.org/10.4135/9781412991841.

Stiles, Derek R. "Pictorial Representation." In *Essential Guide to Qualitative Methods in Organizational Research*, edited by Catherine Cassel and Gillian Symon, 107–119. Thousand Oaks, CA: SAGE, 2004. https://doi.org/10.4135/9781446280119.

Tighe, David. "Worldwide Revenue of Major Toy Companies in 2021 (in Million U.S. Dollars)." *Statista*, July 27, 2022. www.statista.com/statistics/241241/revenue-of-major-toy-companies-worldwide/.

Willig, Carla. *Introducing Qualitative Research in Psychology*. 3rd ed. New York: Open University Press, 2013.

5 Nostalgia-oriented purchase – results of the quantitative research

5.1 Methodology of a quantitative research

For the purpose of the study, the method of indirect communication with the respondents, that is, consumers representing generations X, Y, and Z, was applied using a survey questionnaire (see Appendix). The study has utilised Computer-Assisted Web Interviewing (CAWI) technique using an online self-administered questionnaire and Pen-and-Paper Personal Interview (PAPI) technique using a self-administered paper questionnaire. The final version of the survey questionnaire was prepared on the basis of the literature review and the results of qualitative research conducted in 2022.

The selection of the research method and technique was justified, given the specificity of the study topic and the need to include a larger group of respondents. Initially, the CAWI technique was intended to be used as the sole technique. However, the lack of a sufficient number of completed questionnaires has led to the additional application of PAPI technique in order to achieve the desired number of responses. The decision to pursue both CAWI and PAPI methods was determined after a careful appraisal of their advantages and limitations.

This study was conducted among consumers representing generations X, Y, and Z. The limitation of the study to these age groups was due to the fact that these individuals most often make toy purchases for their own children, as gifts, or to satisfy their own needs. Furthermore, individuals from these generations grew up in a time when popular global toy brands were already available on the Polish market. As such, a purposive, stratified sampling method was implemented for this study. The quantitative research was conducted in the first quarter of 2023.

The survey questionnaire contained 11 closed questions. The general data about the respondent, constituting the final part of the questionnaire, counted questions that related to the following details: gender, age, place of residence, work situation, and offspring owned. The questionnaire contained questions corresponding to the following subject areas: factors affecting purchase decisions, type of motivation, attitude, and purchase intention.

DOI: 10.4324/9781003606079-8

The questionnaire included single-choice and multiple-choice questions based on a dichotomous scale and a nominal scale, as well as questions using a 5-point Likert scale. A total of 535 completed survey questionnaires were collected.

The analysis conducted by Grębosz-Krawczyk[1] allowed for the identification of 20 tools for measuring nostalgia developed between 1980 and 2018 and used in marketing research. Early attempts to measure nostalgia were made by Taylor and Konrad,[2] Batcho,[3] and Holbrook.[4] Most of the tools developed in subsequent years were modifications of the tool proposed by Holbrook. In 2002, Pascal et al.[5] developed the Nostalgic Experience Measurement Tool (NOST). In turn, Merchant et al.[6] developed a 34-item tool designed to measure advertising-induced nostalgia. And in 2018, Ford, et al.[7] on the basis of Merchant et al.'s[8] experience developed a 20-item tool to assess positive and negative nostalgia, taking into account the lifetime of the brand. The validation of existing tools relating to nostalgia evoked by advertising, products, the brand, and its elements led the authors to select the chosen items of the tool proposed by Pascal et al.[9] to create the five-item NOST scale. The item NOST_6 was used to verify the respondents' answers. The reasons for such a choice were as follows: the limited number of statements to be assessed, the possibility of using this tool in Polish conditions, and the possibility of applying it to different age groups of respondents. The dedicated questionnaire uses a 5-point Likert scale, in which 1 means 'strongly disagree' and 5 means 'strongly agree' (Table 5.1).

Purchase in the context of toys generally pertains to either gift-giving or buying for self-indulgence. Therefore, the authors have decided to split the operationalisation of 'purchase' into two distinct subscales with the aim of evaluating all the drives correlated to each segment of the construct being measured.

Gifts are anything tangible or intangible that can be bestowed as presents. A special meaning is imbued to these objects through bonds of the social connection one establishes with other human beings.[10] Throughout the course of history and across diverse cultures, the act of gift-giving has been regarded as an integral component of social conventions,[11] thereby playing a crucial role

Table 5.1 Operationalisation of nostalgia

Construct	*Operational measurement of the construct*	*Author(s) and year*
Nostalgia	'Remind me of the past' 'Help me recall pleasant memories' 'Make me reminisce about a previous time' '. . . are a pleasant reminder of a past' 'Bring back memories of good times from the past' 'Reminds me of good times in the past'	Pascal et al., 2002; Muehling and Pascal, 2011; Muehling et al., 2014; Ju et al., 2017

in establishing and maintaining social relationships. Gift exchange is a form of micro-ritual focused on creating continuity with the past and thus on forging new memories.[12] Csikszentmihalyi and Rochberg-Halton[13] ascertained that gifts are specific types of possessions liable to sacralisation. Stripped of their utilitarian value, these objects convey the hidden message a giver wishes to transmit to the receiver. According to Belk,[14] the parental decision to purchase a specific toy for a child is dictated mostly by their expectations they wish to communicate. Therefore, it is true that such possessions symbolise other people, given their inbuilt expressive statement, thereby allowing individuals to communicate their identity to donors or recipients depending on the situation.[15]

Self-indulgence, on the other hand, involves hedonic motivation – it is more a pleasure for itself rather than to attain a specific objective. Despite this conspicuous carefree character, justifiably referring to compulsive consumption, seldom do people realise that such activities are more profound, thereby involving thoughtful intentions.[16] The predominant themes of self-gifts are those of collecting or reclaiming what has been lost somewhere in the past – some of which have been hinted at during focus group sessions. The meaning such objects communicate to the individual is context-bound. Moreover, these possessions are often regarded as a part of the self because they have been acquired as expressions of personal identity and lifestyle choices.[17] Nevertheless, self-gifts are conceived as a token of tangible recognition, a reward that embodies compensation whether or not a person achieves success or experiences failure in life.[18] In the context of toys and nostalgia, a recurrent theme is that of compensating for a play object that either had been lost in childhood or unsatisfied therein. Specifically, it is a personally symbolic longing for a toy of which ownership was hoped to enhance one's self-concept in the days of youth and thus had more subjective meaning than other toys. A collectible item enables its owner to return to the idealised past, providing him/her with the consolation and comfort he/she needs[19] (Table 5.3).

Attitude was operationalised using the work of Fitzmaurice.[20] In her understanding, attitude is a latent antecedent to consumer behaviour; thus, the

Table 5.2 Operationalisation of gift-giving

Construct	*Operational measurement of the construct*	*Author(s) and year*
Gift-giving	'Have you ever bought a toy from a brand that you know from your childhood as a present for a child?' (If so, please specify how many times it has occurred?) 'Would you like to give a child a toy from a brand you know from your childhood?' 'Are you planning to give a child a toy from a brand you know from your childhood in the near future?'	Belk, 1979; Csikszentmihalyi and Rochberg-Halton, 1981; Kessous et al., 2015; Ward and Chan, 2015

Table 5.3 Operationalisation of self-gifts

Construct	*Operational measurement of the construct*	*Author(s) and year*
Self-gifts	'Have you ever bought a toy from a brand that you remember from your childhood (in a renewed or original edition) for yourself?' (If so, specify how many times this has occurred). 'Would you like to buy a toy from a brand that you remember from your childhood for yourself?' 'Are you intending to buy a toy from a brand that you remember from your childhood for yourself? (in the near future)'	Mick and Demoss, 1990; Sherry et al., 1995; Belk et al., 2003; Kessous et al., 2015

attitudinal reaction is situationally bound and is triggered at the time of exposure to the stimuli. Given its multifaceted complexity, much endeavour[21] has been employed by social scholars to provide a coherent definition of attitude that would encompass all the essential characteristics of the concept.[22] Fishbein and Ajzen[23] embraced the following view of the concept: an attitude is 'a function of one's salient beliefs at a given point in time'. Continuing in this vein, MacKenzie and Lutz[24] defined attitude as 'a learned predisposition to respond to a particular stimulus during a particular exposure occasion'. This depiction conveys Fishbein's[25] notion that attitude is learnt, reflects the subject's general feeling on a bipolar evaluative dimension, and indicates a relationship between attitude and behaviour. From a branding perspective, Keller[26] identified brand attitude as a cornerstone of marketing. Attitudes towards a particular brand evince consumers' evaluations and circumspection involving a judgement about that brand. Moreover, they are comprehensive assessments of the brand through the prism of 'perceived quality'[27] and the benefits it produces – whether utilitarian (acquired through interaction with the brand) or image-related (fantasising about the branded product).[28] It follows, therefore, that when consumers are sentimentally attached to a nostalgic toy brand, they can also have a strong positive attitude towards it.

According to Park et al.,[29] attitude is characterised as the degree of favourability or unfavourability a brand holds. With this in mind, similarly to Fitzmaurice,[30] three semantic differential items were included to assess the respondents' attitudes towards toy brands from one's childhood (with 5-point scale, where 1 meant 'definitely unfavourable' and 5 'definitely favourable') (Table 5.4).

The final section of the questionnaire comprised a table with items, each corresponding to different types of motivations presented in Chapter 3 of this monograph. Respondents were asked to rate these eight statements using a 5-point Likert scale, in which 1 means 'strongly disagree' and 5 means 'strongly agree' (Table 5.5).

Table 5.4 Operationalisation of brand attitude

Construct	*Operational measurement of the construct*	*Author(s) and year*
Brand attitude	'My attitude towards toy brands* from my childhood is . . .' 'My associations with the toy brands I knew during my childhood are . . .' 'The first thought that comes to mind about the toy brands from my childhood is . . .'	Fishbein and Ajzen, 1975; Aaker, 1996; Fitzmaurice, 2005; Keller, 2008; Park et al., 2010

Table 5.5 Types of motivation

Questionnaire statements	*'I pay attention to the included accessories and the movable elements of the toy'*	*'I want to follow an unfulfilled childhood dream'*
Corresponding types of motivation	Utilitarian	Hedonic
Questionnaire statements	'I will spontaneously opt for the toy that catches my eye the most'	'I will buy exactly what a child wishes to get'
Corresponding types of motivation	Intrinsic	Extrinsic
Questionnaire statements	Popularity of the toy brand	'I will buy toys that are new, i.e., that have recently become available on the market'
Corresponding types of motivation	Low stimulation	High Stimulation
Questionnaire statements	'I buy the same toys as my friends'	'I will buy any toy, just so a child gets something'
Corresponding types of motivation	Social	Fear

Additionally, six questions concerning factors affecting the toy purchase were included. During both the design and implementation of the survey, care was taken to adhere to ethical principles of conduct. Respondents' rights as individuals were protected during the survey. Participation in the survey was voluntary; it was anonymous, and all personal information was secured. Respondents were not informed of the actual purpose of the study. In addition, in order to ensure the high quality of research, the questionnaire was verified by carrying out a preliminary pilot study conducted in the first quarter of 2023 on a group of 25 Polish respondents. Data were analysed with IBM SPSS Statistics.

5.2 Characteristics of respondents

A total of 535 respondents participated in the study. It was identified that the study's sample was predominantly female, with women representing 72.7% (n = 389) of the total respondents, while nearly 27.3% were male (n = 146). The discrepancy between male and female subjects was apparent in all three generations under examination. Most respondents were within the 1981–1996 cohort (n = 238), which constituted 44.5% of the total study population. Generation Z was the second most represented cohort (n = 212), with a sex ratio comparable to that in Millennials.

In terms of employment status, the two predominant groups were students and people working full-time (n = 241 and n = 240, respectively). Understandably, the bulk of those currently employed were from generations X and Y, whereas the largest student population was from Generation Z. None of the 535 individuals who finished the survey were retired or receiving a disability pension. Notably, one female respondent in the 1965–1980 age group admitted to being unemployed. In comparison, ten people, primarily females (n = 8), were unemployed for other reasons.

The main objective of toys is to be presented as gifts to children. With this in mind, an inquiry regarding parenthood was included. Nearly 65% of the

Table 5.6 Professional situation of respondents

Professional situation	*Frequency*					
	1965–1980		*1981–1996*		*1997+*	
	Male	*Female*	*Male*	*Female*	*Male*	*Female*
FT empl	25	48	38	114	3	12
PT empl	2	3	2	7	3	4
Student	0	1	16	35	56	133
Jobless	0	1	0	0	0	0
Parental leave	0	0	0	22	0	0
Unemp (other)	1	4	0	4	0	1
Total	28	57	56	182	62	150

Table 5.7 Having an offspring

Family status	*Frequency*		*Per cent*	
	Male	*Female*	*Male*	*Female*
No children	105	242	19.63%	45.23%
Children under 12 years	28	111	5.23%	20.75%
Children aged 12–17	11	33	2.06%	6.17%
Children in legal age	3	14	0.56%	2.62%

respondents (n = 347) stated that they did not have children at the time of taking part in the study. Twelve respondents (2%) reported that they had children in at least two of the three given age groups (e.g., a child under 12 years old and an adult child), thereby indicating the hallmarks of multigenerational families.

Despite the divergence in parenthood status, the authors were able to evaluate the two dimensions of the gift 'purchase' operationalisation (gift-giving and self-gifts).

Table 5.8 provides the descriptive statistics for the five items chosen to measure the construct of nostalgia and its attitude towards the toy brands from one's personally experienced childhood. In order to assess nostalgia, a translated version of the NOST scale developed by Pascal et al.[31] was applied. Due to the linguistic issues, which resulted in obtaining similar-sounding statements, the scale used in the present study was reduced to six items, of which one (Nost_6) has been used in the final analysis to confirm the respondents attention. This approach seems reasonable since, as measured by coefficient alpha, its reliability across the 535 respondents was excellent at $\alpha = 0.945$ with an average corrected item-total correlation of $r = 0.85$. For the purpose of this study, the authors adopted qualitative descriptors recommended by Taber[32] (0.93–0.94 as 'excellent') to provide a valid interpretation of the calculated alpha value.

On a scale from 1 (strongly disagree) to 5 (strongly agree), each measure corresponding to the concept of nostalgic feelings being attached to the toy brands that defined one's childhood was rated in a favourable way, thus surpassing the mean score of 4.218 on average. At a glance, males appeared to have a more intense nostalgic reaction than females, specifically as displayed in the first two and the fifth item. This result is consistent with a study by Holbrook and Schindler,[33] indicating that males' nostalgia is expressed through latency, requiring an adjusted stimulus in order to be invoked. Following in this vein, toys that are

Table 5.8 Nostalgic attitude of customers by gender

		Nost_1	*Nost_2*	*Nost_3*	*Nost_4*	*Nost_5*
Female	*Mean*	4.208	4.234	4.201	4.172	4.221
	Median	5.000	5.000	5.000	5.000	5.000
	N	389	389	389	389	389
	SD	1.096	1.089	1.117	1.128	1.088
Male	*Mean*	4.315	4.308	4.212	4.206	4.260
	Median	5.000	5.000	5.000	4.000	5.000
	N	146	146	146	146	146
	SD	1.015	0.899	1.065	0.996	0.955
Total	*Mean*	4.237	4.254	4.204	4.181	4.232
	Median	5.000	5.000	5.000	5.000	5.000
	N	535	535	535	535	535
	SD	1.075	1.040	1.102	1.093	1.052

targeted towards boys (Power Rangers action figures, LEGO *Bionicle*, Pokémon collectible merchandise, etc.) and make references to their autobiographical past can be regarded as such dormant stimuli. However, a statistically significant difference in nostalgia proneness between genders was not found and is therefore not discussed further. Similar conclusions, though suggesting females to be more nostalgia-prone than men, have been reported in the literature.[34]

Table 5.9 shows the descriptive statistics of nostalgic intensity among the three age cohorts. The highest scores were obtained within the post-Millennial cohort, with the average score value for each item surpassing 4.306. In addition, these values seem to decrease with age: the older the subjects, the lower their mean scores. Lambert-Pandraud and Laurent[35] found that older consumers tend to be more inclined to buy long-standing brands rather than those favoured by younger people, hence their enhanced nostalgic propensity. On the basis of the results of the present study, it seems to be just the opposite.

To justify this finding, Holbrook and Schindler[36] revealed that individuals may differ in their attitudes towards the past, with a specific emphasis on the discrepancies occurring in the degrees of nostalgia propensity between cohorts rather than age groups. That is, the subject's nostalgic attitude appears to be more profound towards objects from the past that were relatively new (young) at the time of interaction.

5.3 Toy purchase behaviour

Gift-giving behaviour during toy purchase

Gift-giving is a common practice inscribed in our culture of interpersonal interactions. Conceptualised as a rhetorical gesture shaping and strengthening social relationships, gifts are often regarded as integrators of various social

Table 5.9 Nostalgic attitude of customers by age groups

		Nost_1	*Nost_2*	*Nost_3*	*Nost_4*	*Nost_5*
1965–1980	*Mean*	3.988	4.012	4.035	4.177	4.118
	Median	4.000	4.000	4.000	4.000	4.000
	N	85	85	85	85	85
	SD	1.220	1.118	1.149	1.093	1.085
1981–1996	*Mean*	4.223	4.248	4.202	4.076	4.223
	Median	5.000	5.000	5.000	4.000	5.000
	N	238	238	238	238	238
	SD	1.070	1.088	1.155	1.174	1.066
1997+	*Mean*	4.354	4.359	4.274	4.302	4.288
	Median	5.000	5.000	5.000	5.000	5.000
	N	212	212	212	212	212
	SD	1.003	0.936	1.017	0.985	1.024

behaviours. Toys are specific types of tangible objects, of which the aspect, apart from the perceived utilitarian utility of play, is their ability to be presented as a gift to a child.

When it comes to discussing gender-related patterns in gift-giving, research indicates that women are primary gift donors,[37] especially when it comes to buying toys for children, which is logical, given the assumption whereby gifts are expressive statements underscoring the significance of the emotional bond between the giver and the recipient (such as between the mother and her children). A study by Fischer and Arnold,[38] for example, confirmed statistically significant differences between genders in the number of gifts given. Hence, women are more involved in purchasing gifts such as toys. However, as shown later, the study also found that men exhibiting feminine qualities are more inclined to gift-giving toy purchase behaviour rather than men with more conservative attitudes.

Table 5.10 presents descriptive statistics for gift-giving toy purchase behaviour with respect to sex. Overall, the women who have purchased a toy as a present at least once accounted for 72.1% of the entire sample; therefore, they are more involved in the gift-giving process. Moreover, the frequency of females who answered '3 to 5 times' and 'more than 6 times' in terms of purchasing toys for gift purposes was virtually homologous (93/97). Nonetheless, a statistically significant difference in gender involvement in gift-giving behaviour was not found and is therefore not discussed further.

Table 5.11 shows descriptive statistics for gift-giving toy purchase behaviour according to age cohorts. As one can see, these results are logical since

Table 5.10 Gift-giving behaviour during the purchase of a toy by gender

	Female		*Male*	
	Frequency	*Per cent*	*Frequency*	*Per cent*
'Never'	93	23.9%	31	21.2%
'1–2'	106	27.2%	36	24.7%
'3–5'	93	23.9%	54	37.0%
'6+'	97	24.9%	25	17.1%

Table 5.11 Gift-giving predisposition by age group during toy purchases

	1965–1980		*1981–1996*		*1997+*	
	Frequency	*Per cent*	*Frequency*	*Per cent*	*Frequency*	*Per cent*
'Never'	9	10.6%	39	16.4%	76	35.8%
'1 to 2'	24	28.2%	63	26.5%	55	25.9%
'3 to 5'	29	34.1%	64	26.9%	54	25.5%
'6+'	23	27.1%	72	30.3%	27	12.7%

the frequencies for 'never purchased' decrease with the progressing age of the respondents, indicating that older individuals are eventually involved in the ritual of gift-giving, which embraces buying toys for children. Gifts are context-bound; thus, they communicate the relationship between the actors involved. Further, through gift-giving, the donor is able to convey positive emotions such as love for the recipient, but when one takes into account the definition of Beatty et al.,[39] whereby a gift (a toy) is a fulfilment of one's obligation, the conveyance of sustaining traditions that build memories (as during Christmas) is even more markedly evident.

Self-gift behaviour during toy purchase

Sherry and McGrath's[40] ethnographical study has introduced the notion of self-gift as 'a present from me to me'. Indulging oneself in self-gifts reflects the 'little kid within every grown-up'. This commonly repeated justification conveys the mood-regulatory functions of purchasing self-gifts. Mood regulation incorporates a set of behavioural patterns that are consciously initiated in order to maintain empowering aspects of mood that contribute positively to their self-concepts. In this regard, toys seem to fit perfectly into this concept. Mick and DeMoss[41] suggested that individuals who have financial security and live alone have a higher propensity to engage in self-gift behaviours.

Indubitably, consumerism opens doors to many behaviours that enable individuals to muster their emotions; the leading one is self-gift purchasing behaviour.[42] Buying toys for oneself as gifts signifies an achievement context, and its direction depends on the nature of the achievement outcome and the meaning imbued for the outcome, whether or not it is a success or failure.[43] Toys can be particularly meaningful in this context, as they often hold sentimental value and evoke childhood memories that can contribute to positive emotions and self-concepts. Only the possessor is aware of the significance such an object carries.

Table 5.12 provides descriptive statistics for self-gift toy purchase behaviour with respect to sex. The results indicate that only 47.66% of the total respondents have acquired such a self-gift at least once in their lifetime. It is a paradoxical outcome, bearing in mind the account of personal stories disclosed in the focus group discussions, which revealed a tendency among participants to seek out toys as a way of fulfilling unmet childhood desires. Specifically, those were males that were more likely to share this motive. Of 146 male subjects participating in the study, only 41.8% reported acquiring toys in a renewed or original edition, of which worshipped specialness derives from reminiscing a specific moment from the past they wish to preserve. Women, on the other hand, were more likely to buy a toy for themselves (49.9%).

Table 5.13 displays descriptive statistics for self-gift toy purchase behaviour with age cohorts as a grouping variable. Among the three groups, a

Table 5.12 Self-gift predisposition during toy purchases by gender

	Female		*Male*	
	Frequency	*Per cent*	*Frequency*	*Per cent*
'Never'	195	50.1%	85	58.2%
'1–2'	102	26.2%	28	19.2%
'3–5'	47	12.1%	20	13.7%
'6+'	45	11.6%	13	8.9%

Table 5.13 Self-gift predisposition during toy purchases by age groups

	1965–1980		*1981–1996*		*1997+*	
	Frequency	*Per cent*	*Frequency*	*Per cent*	*Frequency*	*Per cent*
'Never'	56	65.9%	120	50.4%	104	49.1%
'1–2'	19	22.4%	51	21.4%	60	28.3%
'3–5'	6	7.1%	33	13.9%	28	13.2%
'6+'	4	4.7%	34	14.3%	20	9.4%

predisposition to self-indulgence was found predominantly in the Millennial and post-Millennial generations. Nearly every second respondent within these cohorts (49.6% and 50.9%, respectively) has acquired a revived nostalgic edition of a toy from his/her childhood for the purposes of their own. Once more, the results demonstrated the impact of communism on Gen Xers, as 65.9% never purchased a toy from a brand they had not been playing with due to the economic barriers imposed on Western products (such as *Barbie, LEGO, My Little Pony,* and *Transformers*), which has been brought up during the focus groups.

The Mann-Whitney test was used to assess differences between genders. From these data, it can be concluded that predisposition to buy toys as self-gifts was statistically significantly higher in females than in males ($U = 21{,}216$, $p = 0.001$).

5.4 Factors influencing toy purchase

The following section discusses factors influencing purchase decisions in terms of acquiring a toy product, such as price, brand awareness, perceived quality, positive associations, perceived educational value, and repetitive behaviour (hereby seen as 'buying the same brands all the time').

Table 5.14 provides descriptive statistics of mean scores for factors affecting the purchase of the nostalgic toy with respect to sex. The most important factor for both males and females was the quality of the toy, with a total average

Table 5.14 Factors affecting purchase decision by gender

		Price	*Brand awareness*	*Quality*	*Positive associations*	*Educational value*	*Routine purchase*
Female	*Mean*	4.175	3.890	4.666	4.131	4.360	2.504
	Median	4.000	4.000	5.000	4.000	5.000	2.000
	N	389	389	389	389	389	389
	SD	0.966	0.977	0.615	0.790	0.893	1.188
Male	*Mean*	4.185	4.192	4.637	4.171	3.671	2.932
	Median	4.000	4.000	5.000	4.000	4.000	3.000
	N	146	146	146	146	146	146
	SD	0.947	0.816	0.562	0.755	1.221	1.301
Total	*Mean*	4.178	3.972	4.658	4.142	4.172	2.621
	Median	4.000	4.000	5.000	4.000	4.000	2.000
	N	535	535	535	535	535	535
	SD	0.960	0.945	0.600	0.780	1.039	1.233

mean score of 4.658 (SD = 0.600). There were no differences in the scores between men and women for this item. Additionally, 'price' (M = 4.178) and 'educational value' (4.172) were the second and third items with the highest mean scores, respectively. One of the indicators determining whether or not brand loyalty occurs is price premium, which is often explained as the amount a customer is going to pay for the product from one brand over another.[44] To be sure, in order to perform price premium analysis, the study would have had to include a benchmark between the focal toy brands to provide valid conclusions. Nevertheless, the overall results for price suggest that the subjects involved in the study display tendencies towards choosing cheaper alternatives within the same toy product categories.

Females look for educational values in a toy (M = 4.360), which is a logical finding given the nurturing commitment, as exhibited in feminine behaviour in promoting children's development, and toys are specifically apt for fostering creativity. On the contrary, men pay attention to the awareness of the brand (M = 4.192), and given slightly better scores on 'routine purchases' (M = 2.932 as opposed to M = 2.504 in females), it might be contended that males epitomise the 'shopping as work'[45] value inherent in the utilitarian shopping motivation. This means that a toy would be acquired in an efficient and task-related manner. Even if a male individual does not buy a toy on the first try, the intelligence gathered during the process (e.g., brand names, current trends, price tag) is well regarded as a reward.[46]

Across the three age cohorts, 'quality' was identified to be the most significant determinant in the first place. Overall, the results seem to be logical as the respondents purchase more toys with progressing age, hence the highest mean scores for routine purchases in the Gen Xers (M = 3.294) and the lowest in Generation Z (M = 2.448). Of particular importance were the differences in the impact of subsequent factors beyond 'quality' on making decisions to purchase toys in Millennials and post-Millennials. Specifically, Millennials exhibited an increased tendency to pursue educational values in a toy in the second place (M = 4.420), while Generation Z focused more on the price and favourable associations towards a brand, thereby indicating the egocentric mindset of younger respondents. Furthermore, unlike older respondents, these two age cohorts appear to be the most price-sensitive when it comes to acquiring a toy from a specific brand, which results in sporadic rather than routine purchases.

Table 5.15 displays descriptive statistics of mean scores for factors affecting the purchase of the nostalgic toy with respect to the parental status of respondents. The toy's perceived quality was a prevalent indicator of a toy purchase among the respondents who had children and those who had not. The first thing that catches the eye is that brand awareness fell short to be considered even in the second place, as opposed to when data were grouped with respect to cohort or gender. Regardless, the mean score values for the subjects' awareness of the brand did not differ markedly between the categorical variables referred to above. As a logical consequence of having offspring, the respondents who were parents, in addition to 'quality', were casting around for toys that encapsulate educational values (M = 4.590), while those without children focused on price (M = 4.233) and positive associations towards the brand (M = 4.187).

The non-parametric Kruskal-Wallis test was employed to assess differences among age cohorts. A significance level of 0.05 was used throughout the analysis. The result showed that there was a statistically significant difference in mean scores between the three age groups for 'quality' $\chi^2(2) = 16.877$, $p = 0.001$, 'educational value' $\chi^2(2) = 69.136$, $p = 0.001$, and 'routine purchase' $\chi^2(2) = 23.794$, $p = 0.001$.

The Mann-Whitney test revealed that the parental status of the respondents had a statistically significant effect on the factors influencing the purchase of a toy. Thus, respondents with children focused on the quality of the toy (U = 29,079.5, $p = 0.009$), followed by its educational values (U = 22,363, p =

Table 5.15 Factors affecting purchase decision according to parental status

		Price	*Brand awareness*	*Quality*	*Positive associations*	*Educational value*	*Routine purchase*
With children	*Mean*	4.075	4.011	4.761	4.059	4.590	2.718
	Median	4.000	4.000	5.000	4.000	5.000	2.000
	N	188	188	188	188	188	188
	SD	1.005	0.884	0.464	0.860	0.618	1.250
Without children	*Mean*	4.233	3.951	4.602	4.187	3.945	2.568
	Median	4.000	4.000	5.000	4.000	4.000	2.000
	N	347	347	347	347	347	347
	SD	0.931	0.977	0.656	0.731	1.145	1.223

0.001), whereas those without children took into account the toy's quality ($U = 29{,}079.5$, $p = 0.009$) and its price ($U = 29{,}500.5$, $p = 0.046$).

5.5 Consumer motivations engaged during the toy buying process

The following section provides an overview of key findings and insights concerning various types of consumer motivations, which were previously reviewed in Chapter 3, and their impact on the participatory subjects in the event of having to make a toy purchase.

Of all motivations that were selected for the purpose of the present study, the three that people were mostly driven by were utilitarian motivation ($M = 3.778$), extrinsic motivation ($M = 3.684$), and low stimulation ($M = 3.105$). With respect to sex, the mean scores for these items were nearly identical (Table 5.16). Interestingly, the respondents were definitely not incited by fear, as was conveyed in the sentence '*I will buy any toy, just so a child gets something*'; hence, the respondents put some considerable effort into the process of selecting and buying a toy that is believed to be well tailored for the child's needs. And this, in turn, does reflect the motive of shopping portrayed as a mission, thereby invoking utilitarian motivation.

Similarly to what has been observed in males and females, the generations X and Y respondents seemed to be mostly driven by utilitarian motivation ($M_{GenX} = 4.024$; $M_{GenY} = 3.773$), followed by extrinsic motivation ($M_{GenX} = 3.612$; $M_{GenY} = 3.656$) and low stimulation ($M_{GenX} = 3.471$; $M_{GenY} = 2.983$), respectively. In a stark contrast, the respondents within the Generation Z cohort were predominantly influenced by extrinsic motivation in the first place ($M_{GenZ} = 3.745$). Once more the results hinted at the apparent advantage of utilitarian motivation over hedonic motivation and extrinsic over intrinsic (Table 5.17).

All age groups unanimously agreed that the selection of a nostalgic toy, whether or not as a present for their own child, someone else's child, or themselves, should be tailored to answer the recipient's needs. Hence, the mean scores for fear motivation were the lowest. Worth noting is the perceived gradual increase in scores for both utilitarian and hedonic motivation as the age of the respondents progresses.

Higher mean scores were observed for 'low stimulation' motivation than for 'high stimulation' motivation ($M_{low\_stm} = 3.104$ vs. $M_{high\_stm} = 2.794$), which indicates that the respondents are attached to specific trusted brands, which is logical for the purpose of the current study. A nostalgic customer expresses loyalty, perhaps the most crucial of Aaker's[47] four assets, incorporating the concept of brand equity; hence, they choose a particular brand over others offered on the market no matter what. Males had higher mean scores than females for both types of motivation. This behavioural tendency correlates with the routine purchase behaviour as was conveyed in the sentence '*I always*

Table 5.16 Overview of motivations' impact on purchasing toys by gender

		Low stimulation	*High stimulation*	*Utilitarian*	*Hedonic*	*Social*	*Fear*	*Intrinsic*	*Extrinsic*
Female	*Mean*	3.054	2.699	3.776	2.478	2.257	1.653	2.841	3.684
	Median	3.000	3.000	4.000	2.000	2.000	1.000	3.000	4.000
	N	389	389	389	389	389	389	389	389
	SD	1.223	1.182	1.074	1.319	1.122	1.043	1.336	1.058
Male	*Mean*	3.240	2.884	3.781	2.966	2.247	1.719	2.870	3.685
	Median	3.000	3.000	4.000	3.000	2.000	1.000	3.000	4.000
	N	146	146	146	146	146	146	146	146
	SD	1.199	1.189	1.007	1.377	1.184	1.009	1.176	0.945
Total	*Mean*	3.105	2.750	3.778	2.611	2.254	1.671	2.849	3.684
	Median	3.000	3.000	4.000	2.000	2.000	1.000	3.000	4.000
	N	535	535	535	535	535	535	535	535
	SD	1.218	1.185	1.055	1.351	1.138	1.033	1.293	1.027

Table 5.17 Overview of motivations' impact on purchasing toys by age group

		Low stimulation	*High stimulation*	*Utilitarian*	*Hedonic*	*Social*	*Fear*	*Intrinsic*	*Extrinsic*
1965–1980	*Mean*	3.471	3.118	4.024	3.024	2.235	1.882	2.965	3.612
	Median	4.000	3.000	4.000	3.000	2.000	1.000	3.000	4.000
	N	85	85	85	85	85	85	85	85
	SD	1.278	1.401	1.058	1.447	1.306	1.295	1.401	1.070
1981–1996	*Mean*	2.983	2.777	3.773	2.630	2.231	1.584	2.685	3.656
	Median	3.000	3.000	4.000	2.000	2.000	1.000	3.000	4.000
	N	238	238	238	238	238	238	238	238
	SD	1.232	1.164	1.102	1.368	1.118	0.945	1.265	1.086
1997+	*Mean*	3.094	2.571	3.684	2.425	2.288	1.684	2.986	3.745
	Median	3.000	2.000	4.000	2.000	2.000	1.000	3.000	4.000
	N	212	212	212	212	212	212	212	212
	SD	1.152	1.080	0.988	1.258	1.092	1.002	1.264	0.940

choose the same toy brands'. The Spearman rank correlation analysis revealed a moderate statistically significant correlation between 'low stimulation' and 'routine purchase' ($r_s(146) = 0.466$, $p = 0.001$ in males and $r_s(146) = 0.434$, $p = 0.001$ in females).

All three age cohorts were predominantly motivated by low stimulation over high levels of stimulation. Not surprisingly, the highest mean scores for both types of motivation were reported in the Gen Xers' cohort (M_{low_stm} = 3.470 compared to M_{high_stm} = 3.117). Specifically, this age generation exhibits a high degree of shopping experience, resulting in preferences towards trusted brands. In addition, the mean scores for high stimulation are also the highest among Xers than in Millennials and post-Millennials, thereby reflecting their enhanced shopping activity. Notably, McAlister and Pessemier[48] asserted that sometimes customers should display innovative behaviour manifested in risky purchases of brands unbeknownst to them to avoid negative levels of stimulation. The results of Spearman correlation analysis revealed a strong statistically significant correlation between 'low stimulation' and 'routine purchase' in the 1965–1980 cohort ($r_s(85) = 0.837$, $p = 0.001$) and a moderate statistically significant correlation in the 1981–1996 cohort ($r_s(238) = 0.466$, $p = 0.001$).

Higher mean scores were associated with utilitarian motivation than the hedonic one ($M_{utilitarian}$ = 3.776 in females and $M_{utilitarian}$ = 3.781 in males), which implies that functional factors of the toys, such as accessories and the movable elements of the toy, motivate consumers to purchase a specific toy product.

The Mann-Whitney test indicated a significant effect of hedonic motivation on sex. Specifically, it was found that men are more predisposed to hedonic motivation than women ($U = 22720.5$, $p = 0.001$). This finding seems to be in contrast with a recent study by Wang et al.,[49] which found females to be more predisposed to hedonic consumption than males. Moreover, the present results have already been hinted at in the qualitative part, given the significantly increased involvement of males during focus group discussions.

The mean scores for both utilitarian and hedonic motives seem to continuously increase as the age of the respondents progresses, which is a result of a more refined shopping experience. A possible explanation would be that the experience derived from the innovative behaviour exhibited in experimenting with various brands, irrespective of the reported experience of others,[50] provides the individual with intelligence regarding brands, product range, specifications, and prices, leading to minimum irritation while being in a store. The Kruskal-Wallis test demonstrated statistically significant differences in being driven by hedonic motivation with respect to age cohorts. That is, the older the customer, the more likely he will purchase a toy based on hedonic reaction $\chi^2(2) = 10.473$, $p = 0.001$, which seems logical since as people grow older, they start to generate their own financial resources by means of work; thus, they can afford such special acquisitions.

The mean scores were higher for extrinsic motivation than for the intrinsic one (M_{Total} = 3.684). Interestingly, there was no observed gender effect on the favourability of extrinsic cues over intrinsic ones. The tendency towards extrinsic motivation is apparent when the subject displays low levels of self-determination in terms of making a purchase, or, more likely, because customers focus on a separable outcome such as meeting a child's needs.

Of all three age cohorts, post-Millennials showed the highest scores for both intrinsic and extrinsic motives (M_{Intr} = 2.986 and M_{Extr} = 3.745, respectively). However, these values do not differ much from those obtained among Millennials and Gen Xers. The perceived advantage of extrinsic orientation over intrinsic cues may be interpreted in a seemingly overlooked notion of adjusting to the recipient, which would fit in the context of gift-giving behaviour. Given the conceptualisation of gifts as 'labour of love'[51] and Sutton's[52] anthropological approach that those are significant utilities imbued in the object that one wishes to transmit to the receiver, it follows, therefore, that when extrinsically motivated, an individual by an act of donating a nostalgic toy may strengthen a relationship with loved ones. Thus, the possibility of the individual's predisposition to walk down memory lanes increases once the object is subjected to consumer sacralisation, as referred to in the works of Csikszentmihalyi and Rochberg-Halton.[53]

When it comes to intrinsically motivated behaviour, the mean scores are nearly the same between the individuals who have never bought a nostalgic toy and those who have made such a purchase at least once. Even when categorised through the act of purchasing toys, the individuals were shown to be driven primarily by extrinsic motivation. According to Chang et al.,[54] customers inclined to extrinsic motivation are concerned with security and display lower levels of self-determination to buy. 'Economic benefits' (e.g., a discount on a toy) is a commonly invoked instigator that makes hesitant customers engage in the purchasing process. Respondents who claimed they have never made a nostalgic purchase of a toy product appear to exhibit slightly higher levels of extrinsic motivation as compared to the individuals who have procured such a toy (M_{Extr} = 3.796 in 'no purchase' vs. M_{Extr} = 3.661 in 'purchase'). However, a statistically significant difference was not found and is therefore not discussed further.

5.6 Positioning of a nostalgic brand in the toy industry

The results of both the qualitative and quantitative studies, in conjunction with the method of critical analysis of domestic and foreign literature, consistently show that successful positioning of a nostalgic toy brand requires a considerable understanding of consumer needs, company capabilities, and competitive actions. In the following section, the authors give some practical recommendations for marketing practitioners and managers.

Positioning is the crux of marketing strategy since it implies that the intention to buy a product is premeditated on the basis of a comparison of the available brand alternatives. This evidence indicates the competitive-oriented impetuses that drive the chosen positioning strategy to target a specifically defined market and the nature of competition.[55] First, marketers need to understand the profile of their consumers and the factors they consider in the decision-making process when buying a product. Second, they have to appreciate the brand's essential difference that engenders a perceived competitive advantage when the brand is being compared with other options existing on market.[56]

Once this frame of reference has been established, it is feasible then to identify the appropriate points of difference (PODs) and points of parity.[57] The former refers to associations that consumers attribute to a specific brand. Specifically, PODs were revealed in the second part of the qualitative study in which the participants had to articulate the first word they had in mind regarding the displayed logos of the focal toy brands. For example, LEGO was associated with the company's enduring *tradition*, whereas My Little Pony was indicative of *equine* toy figures. The latter, on the other hand, are those associations that do not distinguish the brand from its competitors; rather, they are used as a benchmark to underscore the brand's attributes that show its superiority over the competition.[58] The literature describes three types of POPs: category, competitive, and correlational.[59] In order to achieve an advantageous point of parity that will undermine the competitors' point of difference, consumers must have the perception that the brand is indeed outperforming its available alternative. It is therefore necessary to identify what the brands are that the customers compare a specific brand with and what the brand has to offer to potential buyers as a key decision-making factor.[60] In all, the aim of brand positioning is to yield a convincing purchasing rationale, ideally referring to the brand's inheritance, and incepting in customers' minds a sense of perceived authenticity.

The proposed model illustrating the positioning of a nostalgic brand in the toy industry is presented in Figure 5.1.

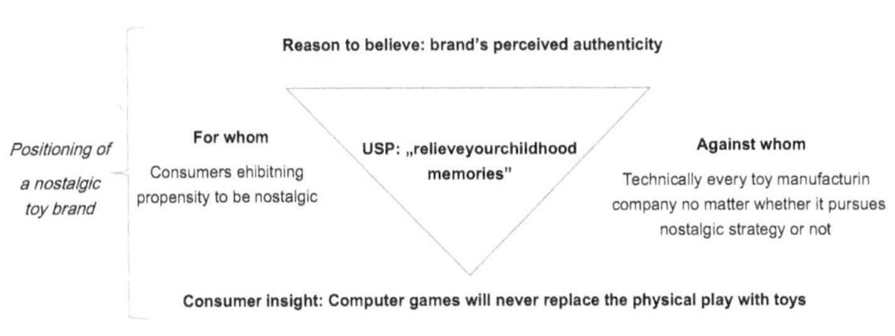

Figure 5.1 The conceptualisation of the positioning of a nostalgic toy brand

As regards the consumers on whom a brand pursuing a nostalgia-oriented positioning strategy directs their efforts, this study showed that of particular concern should be individuals exhibiting a proneness to be nostalgic. The qualitative study has revealed that the structure of the participants' expressed nostalgia encompasses fondness towards personally experienced past, especially childhood, and it may be of either an individual or collective nature. Moreover, such individuals show interest in educational values a toy conveys, as well as its functional attributes; hence, the potential consumers on the Polish market are driven by utilitarian cues of motivation. It was reported that when juxtaposing utilitarian and hedonic motivation, the respondents seemed to be driven more by utilitarian values. In addition, of the eight orientations of consumer motivation, it was the one concerned with instrumental goal-oriented factors that had the highest mean scores in total.

The dominant type of motivation in Ryan and Deci's[61] SDT theory was extrinsic motivation, reflecting the 'shopping as work' theme. Back to the topic of the factors having the effect on the purchase decision in terms of buying a nostalgic toy, this study suggested that the Polish consumers are inclined to perceived quality while being simultaneously sensitive to high prices. In particular, Aaker[62] defines such people as 'price switchers'. Another finding that emerged in the present study was that Polish women were more likely to buy a nostalgic toy for themselves as opposed to men. Nonetheless, focus groups yielded quite contrary conclusions given that those were males, particularly representing generations Y and Z, who disclosed self-gift purchase behaviour, manifested in the form of collecting LEGO sets or in expressing a desire to buy a stimuli variant of the toys (Pokémon, Power Rangers), whose design resembled the toys they had been playing with.

When it comes to defining the competitive frame of reference,[63] technically speaking, every toy manufacturing company may be identified as the brand's competitor, even the one that does not necessarily implement a nostalgia-induced strategy. In the authors' opinion, this finding may be justified in two ways. First, as noted by Chowdhury,[64] brand positioning has little to do with product innovation; rather, it urges to incept a new perception in consumers' minds. In other words, a toy company that wants to compete with a nostalgic brand does not need to go to extraordinary lengths to develop new nostalgic toys, whose designs would resemble its past versions to gain a market share, at least for a while, as long as the brand is aware of its heritage. Secondly, a company may instead approach a nostalgic brand positioning strategy, whereby the past is subjectively fabricated for the needs of the present, referring to the collective identity of target consumers to forge an aura of reputation, thus adding a distinctive value to a product or service. An example includes Hasbro in 2019, who seemed to have followed the nostalgic trend set by LEGO by introducing the *Star Wars*-themed 'anniversary' toy line (celebrating the 20 years since the theatrical release of 'Episode I: The Phantom Menace') to probe the consumers' response in contrast with standard toys. Since then, Hasbro has been releasing the anniversary editions of equine toys from *My Little Pony* and the newly introduced 'Lightning Collection Series' of *Power Rangers* action figures following the acquisition of trademarks and licenses from Saban in 2018.[65] This example illustrates that a toy company may commence a positioning by temporarily manipulating the past so that managers may rely on brand assets they have received from their predecessors thereafter.[66]

Having established the competitive set, marketers must think of a positioning strategy that would fit the purposes of their company. Kapferer[67] provides 11 questions that would help in assessing the choice behind each positioning approach. On the basis of the secondary sources, including the toy manufacturers' websites and catalogues, the authors observed that in relation to the development of a new nostalgic toy product, a common practice involves references to the company's history. Arguably, success is the kind of achievement that evokes positively toned emotional reactions.[68] At the same time, an attempt is made to initiate communication with consumers who have contributed to this success, either indirectly through storytelling with peers, of which narratives conveyed the desire to purchase the branded toy, or directly by the act of acquiring the toy product. In no way, it is possible for a company to succeed in positioning a nostalgic brand without having the concrete piece of history that shaped its identity and status. As summarised earlier, in such a case, a brand could resort to the strategy of creating an artificial past period alluding to the specific events on the basis of the knowledge available at a given moment to make an impression as if the company shared the collective memory of the target consumers. In that case, one may consider the products styled in a retro manner. Nonetheless, the use of nostalgia in the toy industry is evident in the adoption of positioning strategies for nostalgia, which is a unique source of added value to a product or service.[69]

Were it to indicate a single toy manufacturer that has performed the best in terms of evincing its nostalgia-oriented strategy, that would be LEGO. Truly,

Figure 5.2 Forms of storytelling practices in the toy's life cycle

the Danish brick company was the only one of the six brands chosen for this study to conjure up 'nostalgic' as the word the participants in the focus groups associated with the toy brand. Moreover, it was also the one of which word cloud depicted a positively evoked image encapsulating dreams, childhood, play, tradition, and innovation – the core values to which LEGO has been sticking to, and to which it still remains to abide.

The results show that Polish customers expect nostalgic toy brands to introduce new products, which, at first, will have a high degree of innovativeness, thus answering their utilitarian needs. On the other hand, such offerings will refer to the personally or collectively experienced past, thereby satisfying the consumers' nostalgic feelings.

'What is the price of good management?'[70] Such a provocative title was presented by Knudstorp in 2003 before the eyes of the LEGO executive directors.

LEGO® was $800 million in debt. The brick empire was shattering, and voracious private equity firms were soaring like vultures to snag the remaining of the injured family-owned business. With colossal debts almost comparable with its annual sales, the near-bankrupt company seemed destined for the end.[71] Knudstorp was convinced that the company's trouble was not caused in any way by the lack of innovation. He found that the primary cause was not in the allegedly old-fashioned management board, but rather in the poorly defined strategy to create distinctive, desirable offerings at any cost. After spending years pursuing innovation backwards, the brick empire righted its course, aided by a new management team and the basic strength of its product line. Since the Danish PhD took the helm of the company, one can clearly see that throughout the years, consumers have experienced a massive awash of revived versions of their beloved, most desired brick sets (this process has been delineated in Figure 5.3). For example, probably one of the most yearned LEGO sets ever, the *Millennium Falcon*, released for the first time in 2000, has already been recreated nine times.

To confirm that this is not just a coincidence but is also a meticulous positioning strategy of a nostalgic toy brand, another example will be used to illustrate. The very first series of *Bionicle,* featuring the first six defenders of the fictional island of Mata Nui (Tahu, Lewa, Gali, Kopaka, Onua, and Pohatu), has been revived six times since the world premiere in 2001. In this particular case, the managers have adopted a completely different strategy in which nostalgia has met innovation. The creative writers, who invented the compelling story of *Bionicle*, came up with the evolution process of their characters. Through wearing a golden Kanohi mask, the warrior would gain new powers, tougher armour, and updated weaponry yet still remain the same protector of the attributed force of nature. With these ideas in mind, the creators have worked hard to retain the iconic bold design resembling their original appearance so that the consumers would later recognise their heroes on a shop shelf – familiar warriors from childhood wearing a piece of whole new equipment.

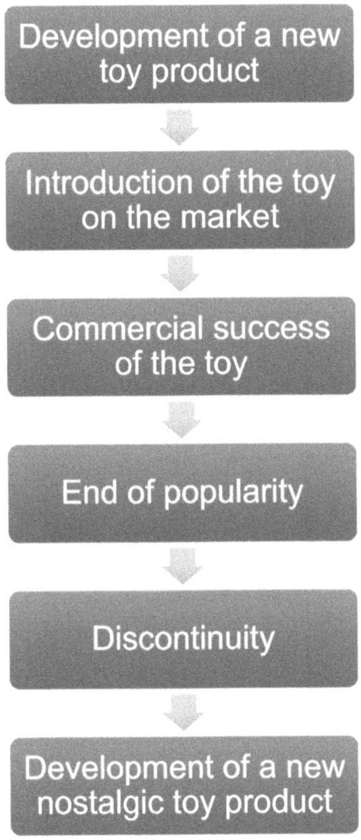

Figure 5.3 Application of the strategy of 'backward innovation' in the toy industry

These recommendations address the direction of marketing activities to evaluate and choose a nostalgic positioning strategy that would establish competitive superiority in the minds of customers and within the toy industry.

Notes

1 Grębosz-Krawczyk, *Nostalgia w Zarządzaniu Marką*, 100.
2 Taylor and Konrad, "Scaling Dispositions Toward the Past", 283–307.
3 Batcho, "Nostalgia: A Psychological Perspective", 131–143.
4 Holbrook, "Nostalgia and Consumption Preferences: Some Emerging Patterns of Consumer Tastes", 245–165.
5 Pascal et al., "The Influence of Evoked Nostalgia on Consumers' Responses to Advertising: An Exploratory Study", 39–49.
6 Merchant and Rose, "Effects of Advertising-Evoked Vicarious Nostalgia on Brand Heritage", 150–165.
7 Ford et al., "The Cross-Cultural Scale Development Process: The Case of Brand-Evoked Nostalgia in Belgium and the United States", 19–29.

8 Merchant and Rose, "Effects of Advertising-Evoked Vicarious Nostalgia on Brand Heritage", 150–165.
9 Pascal et al., "The Influence of Evoked Nostalgia on Consumers' Responses to Advertising: An Exploratory Study", 39–49.
10 Sherry, "Gift Giving in Anthropological Perspective", 159.
11 Ward and Chan, "Gift Giving", 398–399.
12 Belk, "Attachment to Possessions", 45.
13 Csikszentmihalyi and Halton, *The Meaning of Things: Domestic Symbols and the Self*, 92.
14 Belk, "Gift-Giving Behavior", 32.
15 Sherry, "Gift Giving in Anthropological Perspective", 161.
16 Belk et al., "The Fire of Desire: A Multi-Sited Inquiry Into Consumer Passion", 328.
17 Berkman et al., "Valuation as a Mechanism of Self-Control and Ego Depletion", 261.
18 Mick and DeMoss, "Self-Gifts: Phenomenological Insights from Four Contexts", 322.
19 Kessous et al., "Consumer–Brand Relationships: A Contrast of Nostalgic and Non-Nostalgic Brands", 190.
20 Fitzmaurice, "Incorporating Consumers' Motivations into the Theory of Reasoned Action", 911–929.
21 Thurstone, "Attitudes Can Be Measured", 529–554; Allport, "Attitudes", 798–844; Krech and Crutchfield, *Theory and Problems of Social Psychology*.
22 Fishbein and Ajzen, *Predicting and Changing Behavior: The Reasoned Action Approach*, 76.
23 Fishbein and Ajzen, *Belief, Attitude, Intention, and Behavior: An Introduction to Theory and Research*, 22.
24 MacKenzie and Lutz, "An Empirical Examination of the Structural Antecedents of Attitude Toward the Ad in an Advertising Pretesting Context", 49.
25 Fishbein and Ajzen, *Belief, Attitude, Intention, and Behavior: An Introduction to Theory and Research*, 6.
26 Keller, *Strategic Brand Management: Building, Measuring, and Managing Brand Equity*, 166.
27 Aaker, "Measuring Brand Equity Across Products and Markets", 109.
28 Park et al., "Brand Attachment and Brand Attitude Strength: Conceptual and Empirical Differentiation of Two Critical Brand Equity Drivers", 3–4.
29 Park et al., "Brand Attachment and Brand Attitude Strength: Conceptual and Empirical Differentiation of Two Critical Brand Equity Drivers", 1.
30 Fitzmaurice, "Incorporating Consumers' Motivations into the Theory of Reasoned Action", 917.
31 Pascal et al., "The Influence of Evoked Nostalgia on Consumers' Responses to Advertising: An Exploratory Study", 39–49.
32 Taber, "The Use of Cronbach's Alpha When Developing and Reporting Research Instruments in Science Education", 1278.
33 Holbrook and Schindler, "Nostalgic Bonding: Exploring the Role of Nostalgia in the Consumption Experience", 107–127.

34 Holbrook, "Nostalgia and Consumption Preferences: Some Emerging Patterns of Consumer Tastes", 245–256; Holbrook and Schindler, "Age, Sex, and Attitude Toward the Past as Predictors of Consumers' Aesthetic Tastes for Cultural Products", 412–422; Kessous et al., "Consumer–Brand Relationships: A Contrast of Nostalgic and Non-Nostalgic Brands", 187–202.
35 Lambert-Pandraud and Laurent, "Why Do Older Consumers Buy Older Brands: The Role of Attachment and Declining Innovativeness", 113.
36 Holbrook and Schindler, "Market Segmentation Based on Age and Attitude Toward the Past: Concepts, Methods, and Findings Concerning Nostalgic Influences on Customer Tastes", 34.
37 Cheal, *The Gift Economy*.
38 Fischer and Arnold, "More than a Labor of Love: Gender Roles and Christmas Gift Shopping", 342.
39 Beatty et al., "Personal Values and Gift-Giving Behaviors: A Study Across Cultures", 150.
40 Sherry and McGrath, "Unpacking the Holiday Presence: A Comparative Ethnography of Two Gift Stores", 154.
41 Mick and DeMoss, "Further Findings on Self-Gifts: Products, Qualities, and Socioeconomic Correlates", 145.
42 Luomala and Laaksonen, "A Qualitative Exploration of Mood-Regulatory Self-Gift Behaviors", 412.
43 Mick and Faure, "Consumer Self-Gifts in Achievement Contexts: The Role of Outcomes, Attributions, Emotions, and Deservingness", 295–296.
44 Aaker, "Measuring Brand Equity Across Products and Markets", 106–107.
45 Babin et al., "Work and/or Fun: Measuring Hedonic and Utilitarian Shopping Value", 646.
46 Babin et al., "Work and/or Fun: Measuring Hedonic and Utilitarian Shopping Value", 646.
47 Aaker, "Measuring Brand Equity Across Products and Markets", 105–106.
48 McAlister and Pessemier, "Variety Seeking Behavior: An Interdisciplinary Review", 314.
49 Wang et al., "Effects of Hedonic Shopping Motivations and Gender Differences on Compulsive Online Buyers", 129.
50 Midgley and Dowling, "Innovativeness: The Concept and Its Measurement", 235.
51 Fischer and Arnold, "More than a Labor of Love: Gender Roles and Christmas Gift Shopping", 334.
52 Sutton, "A Tale of Easter Ovens: Food and Collective Memory", 160.
53 Csikszentmihalyi and Halton, *The Meaning of Things: Domestic Symbols and the Self*, 92.
54 Meyer-Waarden et al., "The Effects of Purchase Orientations on Perceived Loyalty Programmes' Benefits and Loyalty", 201–225.
55 Keller and Lehmann, "Brands and Branding: Research Findings and Future Priorities", 740.
56 Kapferer, *The New Strategic Brand Management: Advanced Insights and Strategic Thinking*, 176.
57 Keller, *Strategic Brand Management: Building, Measuring, and Managing Brand Equity*, 58.

58 Kotler and Keller, *A Framework for Marketing Management*, 133.
59 Kotler and Keller, *A Framework for Marketing Management*, 133.
60 Kapferer, *The New Strategic Brand Management: Advanced Insights and Strategic Thinking*, 178.
61 Ryan and Deci, "Intrinsic and Extrinsic Motivations: Classic Definitions and New Directions", 54–67.
62 Aaker, *Building Strong Brands*, 22.
63 Kotler and Keller, *A Framework for Marketing Management*, 131.
64 Chowdhury, "An Investigation of Consumer Evaluation of Brand Extensions", 383.
65 Toonkel, "Exclusive: Hasbro to Acquire Power Rangers, Other Franchises from Saban: Sources".
66 Pecot and De Barnier, "Brand Heritage: The Past in the Service of Brand Management", 72–90.
67 Kapferer, *The New Strategic Brand Management: Advanced Insights and Strategic Thinking*, 177.
68 Gladden and Funk, "Understanding Brand Loyalty in Professional Sport: Examining the Link Between Brand Associations and Brand Loyalty", 57–58.
69 Pecot and De Barnier, "Brand Heritage: The Past in the Service of Brand Management", 72–90.
70 Breen and Robertson, *Brick by Brick: How LEGO Rewrote the Rules of Innovation and Conquered the Global Toy Industry*, 69.
71 Rivkin et al., *LEGO (A): The Crisis*, 1–11.

Reference list

Aaker, David A. *Building Strong Brands*. New York: Free Press, 1996.

Aaker, David A. "Measuring Brand Equity Across Products and Markets." *California Management Review* 38, no. 3 (1996): 102–120.

Allport, Gordon W. "Attitudes." In *A Handbook of Social Psychology*, 798–844. Worcester, MA: Clark University Press, 1935.

Babin, Barry J., William R. Darden, and Mitch Griffin. "Work and/or Fun: Measuring Hedonic and Utilitarian Shopping Value." *Journal of Consumer Research* 20, no. 4 (1994): 644–56. https://doi.org/10.1086/209376.

Batcho, Krystine I. "Nostalgia: A Psychological Perspective." *Perceptual and Motor Skills* 80, no. 1 (1995): 131–143. https://doi.org/10.2466/pms.1995.80.1.131.

Beatty, Sharon E., Lynn R. Kahle, and Pamela M. Homer. "Personal Values and Gift-Giving Behaviors: A Study Across Cultures." *Journal of Business Research* 22, no. 2 (1991): 149–157. https://doi.org/10.1016/0148-2963(91)90049-4.

Beatty, Sharon E., Pamela M. Homer, and Lynn R. Kahle. "Problems With VALS in International Marketing Research: An Example From an Application of the Empirical Mirror Technique." *Advances in Consumer Research* 16, no. 2 (1988): 375–380. https://doi.org/10.1177/0092070388016002.

Belk, Russell W. "Gift-Giving Behavior." In *Research in Marketing*, edited by Jagdish N. Sheth, 26–39. Greenwich, CT: JAI Press, 1979.

Belk, Russell W. "Attachment to Possessions." In *Place Attachment*, edited by Irwin Altman and Setha M. Low, 37–62. Boston: Springer, 1992. https://doi.org/10.1007/978-1-4684-8753-4_3.

Belk, Russell W., Güliz Ger, and Søren Askegaard. "The Fire of Desire: A Multi-Sited Inquiry Into Consumer Passion." *Journal of Consumer Research* 30, no. 3 (2003): 326–351.

Berkman, Elliot T., Lauren E. Kahn, and Jordan L. Livingston. "Valuation as a Mechanism of Self-Control and Ego Depletion." In *Self-Regulation and Ego Control*, edited by E. R. Hirt, J. J. Clarkson and L. Jia, 255–279. San Diego: Elsevier Academic Press, 2016.

Breen, Bill, and David Robertson. *Brick by Brick: How LEGO Rewrote the Rules of Innovation and Conquered the Global Toy Industry*. New York: Random House Business Books, 2013.

Cheal, David. *The Gift Economy*. London: Routledge, 1988.

Chowdhury, Md. Humayun Kabir. "An Investigation of Consumer Evaluation of Brand Extensions." *International Journal of Consumer Studies* 31, no. 4 (2007): 377–384. https://doi.org/10.1111/j.1470-6431.2006.00568.x.

Csikszentmihalyi, Mihaly, and Eugene Rochberg-Halton. *The Meaning of Things: Domestic Symbols and the Self*. Cambridge: Cambridge University Press, 1981.

Fischer, Eileen, and Stephen J. Arnold. "More than a Labor of Love: Gender Roles and Christmas Gift Shopping." *Journal of Consumer Research* 17, no. 3 (1990): 333–345. https://doi.org/10.1086/208561.

Fishbein, Martin, and Icek Ajzen. *Belief, Attitude, Intention, and Behavior: An Introduction to Theory and Research*. Reading, MA: Addison-Wesley, 1975. https://doi.org/10.2307/2065853.

Fishbein, Martin, and Icek Ajzen. *Predicting and Changing Behavior: The Reasoned Action Approach*. 1st ed. New York: Psychology Press, 2009. https://doi.org/10.4324/9780203838020.

Fitzmaurice, Julie. "Incorporating Consumers' Motivations into the Theory of Reasoned Action." *Psychology & Marketing* 22, no. 11 (2005): 911–929. https://doi.org/10.1002/mar.20090.

Ford, John B., Altaf Merchant, Anne-Laure Bartier, and Mike Friedman. "The Cross-Cultural Scale Development Process: The Case of Brand-Evoked Nostalgia in Belgium and the United States." *Journal of Business Research* 83 (2018): 19–29. https://doi.org/10.1016/j.jbusres.2017.09.049.

Gladden, James M., and Daniel C. Funk. "Understanding Brand Loyalty in Professional Sport: Examining the Link Between Brand Associations and Brand Loyalty." *International Journal of Sports Marketing and Sponsorship* 3, no. 1 (2001): 54–81. https://doi.org/10.1108/IJSMS-03-01-2001-B006.

Grębosz-Krawczyk, Magdalena. *Nostalgia w Zarządzaniu Marką*. Warsaw: Wydawnictwo C.H. Beck, 2020.

Holbrook, Morris B. "Nostalgia and Consumption Preferences: Some Emerging Patterns of Consumer Tastes." *Journal of Consumer Research* 20, no. 2 (1993): 245–256. https://doi.org/10.1086/209346.

Holbrook, Morris B., and Robert M. Schindler. "Age, Sex, and Attitude Toward the Past as Predictors of Consumers' Aesthetic Tastes for Cultural

Products." *Journal of Marketing Research* 31, no. 3 (1994): 412–422. https://doi.org/10.2307/3152227.

Holbrook, Morris B., and Robert M. Schindler. "Market Segmentation Based on Age and Attitude Toward the Past: Concepts, Methods, and Findings Concerning Nostalgic Influences on Customer Tastes." *Journal of Business Research* 37, no. 1 (1996): 27–39. https://doi.org/10.1016/0148-2963(96)00023-9.

Holbrook, Morris B., and Robert M. Schindler. "Nostalgic Bonding: Exploring the Role of Nostalgia in the Consumption Experience." *Journal of Consumer Behavior* 3, no. 1 (2003): 107–127. https://doi.org/10.1002/cb.127.

Kapferer, Jean-Noël. *The New Strategic Brand Management: Advanced Insights and Strategic Thinking*. London: Kogan Page, 2012.

Keller, Kevin L. *Strategic Brand Management: Building, Measuring, and Managing Brand Equity*. Upper Saddle River, NJ: Pearson/Prentice Hall, 2008.

Keller, Kevin Lane, and Donald R. Lehmann. "Brands and Branding: Research Findings and Future Priorities." *Marketing Science* 25, no. 6 (2006): 740–759. https://doi.org/10.1287/mksc.1050.0153.

Kessous, Aurélie, Elyette Roux, and Jean-Louis Chandon. "Consumer–Brand Relationships: A Contrast of Nostalgic and Non-Nostalgic Brands." *Psychology & Marketing* 32, no. 2 (2015): 187–202. https://doi.org/10.1002/mar.20772.

Kotler, Philip T., and Kevin Lane Keller. *A Framework for Marketing Management*. Boston: Pearson Education Limited, 2016.

Krech, David, and Richard S. Crutchfield. *Theory and Problems of Social Psychology*. New York: McGraw-Hill, 1948. https://doi.org/10.1037/10024-000.

Lambert-Pandraud, Raphaëlle, and Gilles Laurent. "Why Do Older Consumers Buy Older Brands? The Role of Attachment and Declining Innovativeness." *Journal of Marketing* 74, no. 5 (2010): 104–121. https://doi.org/10.1509/jmkg.74.5.104.

Luomala, Harri T., and Martti Laaksonen. "A Qualitative Exploration of Mood-Regulatory Self-Gift Behaviors." *Journal of Economic Psychology* 20, no. 2 (1999): 147–182. https://doi.org/10.1016/S0167-4870(99)00003-3.

MacKenzie, Scott B., and Richard J. Lutz. "An Empirical Examination of the Structural Antecedents of Attitude toward the Ad in an Advertising Pretesting Context." *Journal of Marketing* 53, no. 1 (1989): 49. https://doi.org/10.1177/002224298905300204.

McAlister, Leigh, and Edgar Pessemier. "Variety Seeking Behavior: An Interdisciplinary Review." *Journal of Consumer Research* 9, no. 3 (1982): 311–322. https://doi.org/10.1086/208926.

Merchant, Altaf, and Gregory M. Rose. "Effects of Advertising-Evoked Vicarious Nostalgia on Brand Heritage." *Journal of Business Research* 66, no. 12 (2013): 2619–2625. https://doi.org/10.1016/j.jbusres.2012.05.021.

Meyer-Waarden, Lars, Christophe Benavent, and Herbert Castéran. "The Effects of Purchase Orientations on Perceived Loyalty Programmes' Benefits and Loyalty." *International Journal of Retail & Distribution Management* 41, no. 3 (2013): 201–225. https://doi.org/10.1108/09590551311306255.

Mick, David Glen, and Corinne Faure. "Consumer Self-Gifts in Achievement Contexts: The Role of Outcomes, Attributions, Emotions, and Deservingness." *International Journal of Research in Marketing* 15, no. 4 (1998): 293–307. https://doi.org/10.1016/S0167-8116(98)00006-8.

Mick, David Glen, and Michelle DeMoss. "Self-Gifts: Phenomenological Insights from Four Contexts." *Journal of Consumer Research* 17, no. 3 (1990): 322–332. https://doi.org/10.1086/208560.

Mick, David Glen, and Michelle DeMoss. "Further Findings on Self-Gifts: Products, Qualities, and Socioeconomic Correlates." In *Advances in Consumer Research*, Vol. 19, edited by John F. Sherry Jr. and Brian Sternthal, 140–146. Provo, UT: Association for Consumer Research, 1992.

Midgley, David F., and Grahame R. Dowling. "Innovativeness: The Concept and Its Measurement." *Journal of Consumer Research* 4, no. 4 (1978): 229–242. https://doi.org/10.1086/208701.

Park, C. Whan, Deborah J. MacInnis, Joseph Priester, Andreas B. Eisingerich, and Dawn Iacobucci. "Brand Attachment and Brand Attitude Strength: Conceptual and Empirical Differentiation of Two Critical Brand Equity Drivers." *Journal of Marketing* 74, no. 6 (2010): 1–17. https://doi.org/10.1509/jmkg.74.

Pascal, Vincent, David E. Sprott, and Darrel D. Muehling. "The Influence of Evoked Nostalgia on Consumers' Responses to Advertising: An Exploratory Study." *Journal of Current Issues and Research in Advertising* 24, no. 1 (2002): 39–47.

Pecot, Fabien, and Virginie de Barnier. "Brand Heritage: The Past in the Service of Brand Management." *Recherche et Applications en Marketing (English Edition)* 32, no. 4 (2017): 72–90. https://doi.org/10.1177/2051570717699376.

Rivkin, Jan W., Stefan Thomke, and Daniela Beyersdofer. *LEGO (A): The Crisis, HBS 713–478*. Boston, MA: Harvard Business School Publishing, 2013.

Ryan, Richard M., and Edward L. Deci. "Intrinsic and Extrinsic Motivations: Classic Definitions and New Directions." *Contemporary Educational Psychology* 25, no. 1 (2000): 54–67. https://doi.org/10.1006/ceps.1999.1020.

Sherry, John F., Jr. "Gift Giving in Anthropological Perspective." *Journal of Consumer Research* 10, no. 2 (1983): 157–168. https://doi.org/10.1086/208956.

Sherry, John F., Jr., and Mary Ann McGrath. "Unpacking the Holiday Presence: A Comparative Ethnography of Two Gift Stores." In *Interpretive Consumer Research*, edited by Elizabeth C. Hirschman, 148–167. Provo, UT: Association for Consumer Research, 1989.

Sutton, David. "A Tale of Easter Ovens: Food and Collective Memory." *Social Research* 75, no. 1 (2008): 157–180. https://doi.org/10.1353/sor.2008.0056.

Taber, Keith S. "The Use of Cronbach's Alpha When Developing and Reporting Research Instruments in Science Education." *Research in Science Education* 48, no. 6 (2018): 1273–1296. https://doi.org/10.1007/s11165-016-9602-2.

Taylor, S. Martin, and Victor A. Konrad. "Scaling Dispositions Toward the Past." *Environment and Behavior* 12, no. 3 (1980): 283–307. https://doi.org/10.1177/0013916580123001.

Thurstone, Louise L. "Attitudes Can Be Measured." *American Journal of Sociology* 33, no. 1 (1928): 529–554. https://doi.org/10.1086/214483.

Toonkel, Jessica. "Exclusive: Hasbro to Acquire Power Rangers, Other Franchises from Saban: Sources." *Reuters*, May 1, 2018. Accessed May 1, 2024. www.reuters.com/article/us-sabanentertainment-m-a-hasbro-exclusi-idUSKBN1I23IQ.

Wang, Xuhui, Fayaz Ali, Muhammad Zubair Tauni, Qilin Zhang, and Tanveer Ahsan. "Effects of Hedonic Shopping Motivations and Gender Differences on Compulsive Online Buyers." *Journal of Marketing Theory and Practice* 30, no. 1 (2022): 120–135. https://doi.org/10.1080/10696679.2021.1894949.

Ward, Morgan K., and Cindy Chan. "Gift Giving." In *The Cambridge Handbook of Consumer Psychology*, edited by Michael I. Norton, Derek D. Rucker and Cait Lamberton, 398–418. Cambridge: Cambridge University Press, 2015.

Final conclusions

Although a growing body of research highlights that the bittersweet elements of nostalgia, such as feelings of happiness and sadness, can influence consumer-brand relationships by fostering a perception of brand authenticity, limited attention has been given to the role of nostalgia in shaping brand positioning strategies aligned with consumer motivations. Previous studies suggest that prior exposure to a brand significantly impacts purchasing decisions, indicating that positioning a brand as nostalgic can enhance purchase intentions and bolster brand loyalty. This monograph seeks to provide a comprehensive assessment of the impact of nostalgia on brand positioning on the example of the toy industry, with a focus on brand perception and consumer motivations.

The findings of the primary research reveal that Polish consumers are predisposed to nostalgic reactions while maintaining a pragmatic approach to toy purchases. They prioritise maximising the utility of the product, focusing on its functional features and educational value. Additionally, the results suggest that Polish customers anticipate nostalgic toy brands to launch new products that balance innovation with nostalgia. These offerings should not only address their utilitarian needs through high levels of innovativeness but also evoke personal or collective memories of the past, fulfilling their nostalgic desires.

The study focused on brands owned by the top four companies by global revenue in 2021. Further analysis identified six brands implementing nostalgia-oriented strategies: LEGO, Barbie, Power Rangers, My Little Pony, Pokémon, and Transformers. These brands significantly shaped the childhoods of generations Y and Z. For Generation X, qualitative findings revealed limited recognition of these brands due to the influence of communism in Poland, with LEGO being the only brand familiar to all groups. This highlights an opportunity for future research comparing perspectives from countries unaffected by communist regimes, such as the Netherlands, Denmark, Japan, and the United States.

The findings revealed that Polish consumers generally hold positive attitudes towards nostalgic toy brands, with nostalgic feelings significantly

DOI: 10.4324/9781003606079-9

influencing these attitudes. Consumers' attitudes varied based on their connection to the brand: brands linked to personal childhood memories, such as LEGO, Pokémon, and Power Rangers, evoked strong positive attitudes, particularly among Millennials and post-Millennials. In contrast, attitudes towards unfamiliar toy brands were more reserved, relying heavily on perceived brand identity. Notably, nostalgic feelings were best expressed in a supportive environment, with narratives often personifying the toy. This distinction between personal recollections and generalised perceptions highlights the importance of memory and storytelling in shaping consumer attitudes towards nostalgic brands.

The study found that utilitarian orientation, extrinsic motivation, and low stimulation significantly drive the purchase of nostalgic toys, regardless of whether they are for oneself or as a gift. Instrumental motivation, aligned with the 'shopping as work' concept, highlights Polish consumers' focus on efficiency and ease in purchasing decisions.

Focus group findings revealed self-indulgent behaviour among male participants from generations Y and Z, with men exhibiting a higher predisposition to self-gifting than women. The study also found a dominance of extrinsic motivation over intrinsic, indicating limited interest in nostalgic toys as self-rewards or compensations for unfulfilled childhood desires. The research noted an increase in hedonic motivation with age, consistent with the supposition that financial security and solitary living enhance self-indulgent consumption. Younger respondents, currently more engaged in self-gifting, may increase such purchases as their financial stability grows. Finally, extrinsic motivation also reflects outcomes beyond the toy's instrumental value, such as fulfilling a child's needs.

The results revealed no statistically significant path coefficients between nostalgic attitudes and the inclination to purchase nostalgic toys. This finding aligns with the concept of human motivation, where nostalgia is seen as a response to a stimulus rather than an instigator of goal-oriented action, such as a purchase.

The process of developing an effective brand positioning strategy begins with assessing how well managers understand their brand's past, which serves as a critical foundation. For emerging or revived brands lacking historical achievements, constructing a heritage by referencing the collective history and identity of potential consumers can compensate. Once the brand's past is defined, it is essential to analyse the competitive landscape and understand both actual and potential customers. Effective nostalgic positioning involves identifying points of parity (POPs) and points of difference (PODs). A strong POD may sometimes be outperformed by a competitor's POPs, requiring implicit communication of the brand's superiority within its category. An example is the LEGO brand. This case demonstrates that innovation is present in every toy company, waiting to be leveraged. It shows that emotional branding, particularly through nostalgia, fosters perceptions of authenticity, trust, affection, and loyalty, adding value through longevity and stability.

An important advantage of adopting a nostalgic positioning strategy is its ability to convey a sense of authenticity, offering consumers an escape from the perceived inauthenticity of the modern world. This authenticity fosters trust and emotional attachment to the brand, which translates into increased consumer loyalty. Moreover, positioning a nostalgic brand provides an effective way to revitalise a struggling brand or reintroduce it to the market by leveraging a distinctive heritage that resonates with collective memory, thereby enhancing the brand's reputation.

In conclusion, the conducted literature review and empirical research demonstrated that the toy industry is a highly competitive landscape where nostalgic positioning practices are both present and necessary. The findings highlight that consumer storytelling, which conveys experiences with a toy brand, plays a pivotal role in fostering tribal communities united by shared consumption activities. Membership in such tribes not only shapes nostalgic attitudes, as observed in focus groups, but also influences individuals' intentions to purchase nostalgic toys tied to collective memory. In this process, consumers emerge as active co-creators of value, further enhancing the brand's relevance and emotional appeal.

The studies conducted have some limitations. First, the selection of brands was based on the 2021 global revenue of major toy companies, excluding smaller brands that might also employ nostalgia-focused positioning. Comparing global toy brands with local manufacturers could reveal differences in consumer perceptions. Additionally, Generation X participants showed low familiarity with the selected brands, relying on visual cues like logos, suggesting the need for an ethnographic approach to explore the toys that defined their childhood and cross-generational differences in toy preferences. Lastly, conducting similar studies across different countries could provide insights into varying consumer attitudes and behaviours towards nostalgic brands.

Appendix

Questionnaire survey – English version

1 **Gender:**

□Male □Female

2 **Age group:**

□1965–1980 □1981–1996 □1997+

3 **Place of residence:**

□Residual area □City to 50,000 □City from 50,000 to 150,000
□City from 150,000 to 500,000 □City larger than 500,000

4 **Current employment status:**

□Full-time □Part-time/Freelancer/Contractor □Retired, disabled pensioner □Student
□Unemployed: out of job □Unemployed: on parental leave
□Unemployed for other reasons

5 **Having offspring:**

□No children □Children aged under 12 years old □Children aged between 12 and 17
□Adult children

6 **'Toy brands from my childhood . . .'**

By using the word 'brand' the Author means LEGO, Pokémon, Power Rangers, My Little Pony, Transformers, Barbie, etc. (where 1 means 'strongly disagree' and 5 means 'strongly agree')

'Remind me of the past'	□1 □2 □3 □4 □5
'Help me recall pleasant memories'	□1 □2 □3 □4 □5
'Make me reminisce about a previous time'	□1 □2 □3 □4 □5
'. . . are a pleasant reminder of a past'	□1 □2 □3 □4 □5
'Bring back memories of good times from the past'	□1 □2 □3 □4 □5
'Reminds me of good times in the past'	□1 □2 □3 □4 □5

7 To what extent do you agree with the following statements? *(where 1 means 'strongly disagree' and 5 means 'strongly agree')*

'When I am reminded of the period of my childhood I long to revisit that era'.
□1 □2 □3 □4 □5

'Because I hold the time period of my childhood in high regard, I want to be part of that time period once again'.
□1 □2 □3 □4 □5

'I would like to relive the time period of my childhood because those times are better than present time'.
□1 □2 □3 □4 □5

'I wish I could return to the time period of my childhood'.
□1 □2 □3 □4 □5

8 Finish the following sentence: *(where 1 means 'definitely unfavourable' and 5 means 'definitely favourable')*

'My attitude towards toy brands* from my childhood is . . .'
□1 □2 □3 □4 □5

'My associations with the toy brands I knew during my childhood are . . .'
□1 □2 □3 □4 □5

'The first thought that comes to mind about the toy brands from my childhood is . . .'
□1 □2 □3 □4 □5

9 Please answer to the following questions:

'Have you ever bought a toy from a brand that you know from your childhood as a present for a child?' (If so, please specify how many times it has occurred?) **your own or someone else's child*
□Never □1 to 2 □3 to 5 □6 to 9 □more than 10

'Would you like to give a child a toy from a brand you know from your childhood?'
(where 1 means 'strongly disagree' and 5 means 'strongly agree')
□1 □2 □3 □4 □5

'Are you planning to give a child a toy from a brand you know from your childhood in the near future'?
(where 1 means 'strongly disagree' and 5 means 'strongly agree')
□1 □2 □3 □4 □5

'Have you ever bought a toy from a brand that you remember from your childhood (in a renewed or original edition) for yourself'? (If so, specify how many times this has occurred).
☐Never ☐1 to 2 ☒3 to 5 ☐6 to 9 ☐more than 10

'Would you like to buy a toy from a brand that you remember from your childhood for yourself'?
(where 1 means 'strongly disagree' and 5 means 'strongly agree')
☐1 ☐2 ☐3 ☐4 ☐5

'Are you intending to buy a toy from a brand that you remember from your childhood for yourself? (in the near future)'
(where 1 means 'strongly disagree' and 5 means 'strongly agree')
☐1 ☐2 ☐3 ☐4 ☐5

10 What do you take into account when considering a purchase of a toy? ***(where 1 means 'strongly disagree' and 5 means 'strongly agree')***

Price of the toy	☐1	☐2	☐3	☐4	☐5
Cognisance of the toy brand	☐1	☐2	☐3	☐4	☐5
Quality of the toy	☐1	☐2	☐3	☐4	☐5
Favourable associations with the toy brand	☐1	☐2	☐3	☐4	☐5
Educational value of the toy product	☐1	☐2	☐3	☐4	☐5
I always choose the same toy brands.	☐1	☐2	☐3	☐4	☐5
Popularity of the toy brand	☐1	☐2	☐3	☐4	☐5
I will buy toys that are new, that is, that have recently become available on the market.	☐1	☐2	☐3	☐4	☐5
I pay attention to the included accessories and the movable elements of the toy.	☐1	☐2	☐3	☐4	☐5
I want to follow an unfulfilled childhood dream	☐1	☐2	☐3	☐4	☐5
I buy the same toys as my friends	☐1	☐2	☐3	☐4	☐5
I will buy any toy, just so a child gets something.	☐1	☐2	☐3	☐4	☐5
I will spontaneously opt for the toy that catches my eye the most.	☐1	☐2	☐3	☐4	☐5
I will buy exactly what a child wishes to get.	☐1	☐2	☐3	☐4	☐5